(continued from front flap)

Church, led him to write on the subject for Catholic magazines, and caused him to be chosen as archdiocesan director of mission aid. It also prompted him to promote with Father Price of North Carolina the establishment of Maryknoll by the American hierarchy, to labor with dynamic ardor for the building of the Society in the United States, and to journey throughout the world in the Society's interests.

What of the man behind this career? He has been described as one of the greatest and most charming figures of the Church in America. Daniel Sargent in his gracious style depicts the human and lovable characteristics which underlay his deep and moving principles of action and which combined with them to make this life so remarkable.

Bishop Walsh awakened admiration and affection in all who knew him. Daniel Sargent's biography promises to widen the circle of acquaintanceship immensely and, by the same token, the respect and love for this outstanding Catholic leader in the American scene.

LONGMANS, GREEN AND COMPANY

55 FIFTH AVENUE

NEW YORK

ALL THE DAY LONG

Books by Daniel Sargent

Thomas More
Four Independents
Catherine Tekakwitha
Our Land and Our Lady
Christopher Columbus
All the Day Long

Verse

The Door
The Road to Welles-Perennes
My Account of the Flood
The Song of the Three Children
God's Ambuscade

ALL THE DAY LONG

By DANIEL SARGENT

James Anthony Walsh

COFOUNDER OF MARYKNOLL

LONGMANS, GREEN & COMPANY

NEW YORK :: TORONTO

Cum Permissu Superiorum

Nihil Obstat

ARTHUR J. SCANLAN, S.T.D.
Censor of Books

Imprimatur

✠ FRANCIS J. SPELLMAN, D.D.
Archbishop of New York

September 5, 1941

May He support us all the day long, till the shadows lengthen, and the evening comes, and the busy world is hushed, and the fever of life is over, and our work is done! Then in His mercy may He give us a safe lodging, and a holy rest, and peace at the last.

—CARDINAL NEWMAN

A favorite prayer of Bishop Walsh

Contents

Acknowledgment

THE AUTHOR is glad to say that he is one of those who, face to face, knew Bishop James Anthony Walsh, yet he has had to go for information to those who knew him longer and better, and he has a debt of gratitude to them and to their communicativeness.

He wishes to thank Cardinal O'Connell, of Boston, and numerous priests of the Boston Archdiocese, some of whose names appear in these pages. He has a special debt to Monsignor Duggan, of the Hartford Diocese. He wishes to thank the surviving relatives of Bishop Walsh, especially Mrs. Thomas B. Hughes, his sister, and Mrs. Patrick Tracy, his cousin. He wishes to thank numerous acquaintances of the deceased Bishop. To all of these who gave him of the store of their memory, he owes also an apology. He has taken their reminiscences and given his own interpretation to them, which is the best he could do, but certainly not in every case what they expected.

The author's debt to the Maryknoll Fathers can be so taken for granted that it need not be mentioned. And the same may be said of Mother Mary Joseph and the Maryknoll Sisters. In

their hearts can be found the profoundest understanding of
their leader; in their archives are the records of his most active
years. But for special reasons the debt to Father George C.
Powers of Maryknoll cannot be passed over. Not only did he
possess material; he arranged it. Although the author would
not like to embarrass Father Powers by ascribing to him any
of his own mistakes in fact (which he hopes he has not made),
or any of his personal judgments (which must in the end
remain personal), he does ascribe to him what evidences of
industry and accuracy the book may possess.

Illustrations

ALL THE DAY LONG

The Boy

THIS IS the story of James Anthony Walsh, a man who was allotted his daylight of a lifetime here under our sun, in our country, from 1867 to 1936.

He was the man whom his friends so easily recognized by his eyebrows, arched as if in surprise; by his eyes, in which burned candlelight which sharpened or grew dim; by his lips, which were ready to smile and yet waited.

He was the man who delighted his friends by his reserve and his wit.

He was the man who perplexed them, too, by being so sensitive and yet such a man of action.

He was the man—the priest—who, with Father Thomas Frederick Price, founded the Catholic Foreign Mission Society of America, generally known as "Maryknoll."

But most of all he was the man who, more than any other, had changed the attitude of Catholics in the United States from that of indifference to foreign missions to that of enthusiasm for them.

His daylight of a lifetime began in Cambridge, Massachusetts, on Saint Matthias Day, February 24, 1867. He still

3

slept and knew no more of what his future work should be than any other mother's newborn babe.

The American Civil War had ended two years before. He had never heard of it.

His father was James Walsh, and his mother Hannah Shea Walsh, both of whom had been born in Ireland, in County Cork, and both of whom as children had come to the United States. They had become Americans. He could not see them.

On February 26, two days after his birth, he was wrapped up like a bundle of clothes in order to be taken to his baptism. The parents were Catholics, who believed with an old-fashioned earnestness. They were acutely conscious of their responsibility for the eternal happiness of this little baby who slept, who could not care for himself. The wonder of having a child beginning his eternity with them was still fresh upon them; they had had but one child before. Let there be no delay about the baptism.

Their house stood on Hampshire Street, Cambridge, a mile or so east of Harvard College, which then had no towers and was comparatively inconspicuous. The district at the time was not thickly settled. Indeed it was almost rural, and uncitified. The parents had been brought up in much-more-citified Boston, the capital of Massachusetts and New England's greatest city. But, as a young married couple, they had moved across the tidewater basin of the Charles River, and settled where it was less expensive to live, in the Cambridge which looked across at the gilded dome of the State House on Boston's Beacon Hill. They belonged to Saint Peter's Parish, the church of which had been built of brick thirty-six years earlier by the

Reverend Manassas P. Dougherty at a point where Concord Avenue tops a rise behind Cambridge.

The church was a mile away, and to take the babe to his baptism stood a cab at the door. Amy Walsh, who was to be godmother, carried the infant into the cab. Dennis Shea was to be the other godparent. He also entered the cab, as did the father, who wore a beard which gave him greater antiquity than his years warranted. The name of the precious son had long since been decided on. His elder brother had been called Andrew, after the father's father. This second son they would call simply James—after his father—James Junior—another James.

Off trotted the horse until he came to the muddy, slippery February slope of Concord Avenue. Then he walked. Then he stopped at the rectory. The babe was carefully handed from Amy Walsh to another, while Amy descended, and then back to Amy. The babe slept.

"James, what dost thou ask of the Church of God?" asked Father Dougherty.

"Faith," answered a sponsor.

Father Dougherty trickled water on the baby's forehead, put salt on his tongue, draped a white cloth over his small shoulder, next to his roseate knob of a head, as a robe of innocence; and declared him dead to sin as Christ had died on the Cross.

"James, go in peace, and may the Lord be with thee," terminated Father Dougherty.

A few months later James, the son of James and the grandson of Andrew, took another horse-and-carriage journey. It was across the West Boston Bridge to Boston, to which grander city he was being taken by his parents, there to live in a grander house in Greenwich Park off Columbus Avenue—Number 14. His eyes from time to time opened and reflected the crystal light that came through the cab's windows.

As the years went by, he began to wake up. He found himself surrounded by a certain affluence, which he did not recognize by that or any other name, simply taking it as a matter of course. Greenwich Park was one of those neatly designed rectangular oases which the realtors and architects of twenty years previously had erected in the South End of Boston in imitation of similar parks in London's West End. Number 14 was of brick. It had a flight of a dozen stone steps leading up to its proud front door. The right half of its façade was rounded to give the windows a chance to look not only straight out, but also sideways.

James Walsh, the father, was a man who had made some money. Most of the Irish who had come from the economic ruin of persecuted Ireland had arrived in the United States at an economic disadvantage. There was very little chance for any of them to attain to sudden wealth, for they had no invested capital or inherited land, by which to profit by the country's growing prosperity. Mr. Walsh had begun as a liquor dealer. Although possessing none of the disagreeable qualities of a money getter and absolutely no tendency or qualification to stimulate a taste for too much liquor in others —being a mild, quiet, very neat, dignified, over-temperate, venerably bearded citizen—he nevertheless did make money, and became in his generous way a capitalist, investing some of his gains in lands, from which he hoped for a profit, and others in private loans to friends, from which he hoped against hope for repayment.

Mr. James Walsh owned not only a brick house, but a horse and two carriages, one of them a buggy for two, and the other a carryall which could contain the whole family even as it grew—one, two, three, four, five, six. He bought also a summer cottage at Ocean Spray, Winthrop, to which he would trek annually in the carryall when the bricks in Boston grew redder in the July heat.

The interior of Number 14 Greenwich Park had its amenities, which went well with its owner's prosperity; and over those amenities reigned Mrs. Walsh. In the fight of the Irish to receive an education at home in Ireland, she had fared better than her husband. Her mother had been a valiant woman, who, though left a widow all too soon, had resolutely insisted that her children be educated, cost what it might. Public instruction was Protestant, and she had had to hire a private Catholic tutor to teach by candlelight. Through him her daughter, the future Mrs. Walsh, learned letters and the love of letters. She had herself instructed her daughter in sewing, both coarse and fine, and in embroidery, and had taught her to play the piano. When evil days had come, when it had been necessary to cross the Atlantic, old Mrs. Shea had kept up her high standards. And Mrs. James Walsh, her daughter, was still, in 1870, in Boston, keeping up the tradition.

Young James Walsh, or "Jimmie," as he was called, became aware of the present in 14 Greenwich Park. To a child the present seems eternal. At the age of six he became aware of a world that did not center in his father's house. He went to

school, at the Dwight Public Grammar School on West Spring-
field Street.

With still another world he had grown acquainted: heaven.
He did not die to go there, and he saw it only by analogy in
the form of the great snowy interior of the Jesuit Church of
The Immaculate Conception, on Harrison Avenue, which was
technically not a parish church and yet was the votive church
of the South End. Its interior was splendid with candles and
candelabras, and was sonorous with mighty music. It was un-
earthly in the impassioned attitude of its statued saints as they
gestured ecstatically to Our Lady on the wall behind the altar.
At this church he attended Mass. At this church he attended
Sunday School.

One day when he was nine, a competition in elocution was
held in his school, even as in all the public schools. The
philanthropic Emperor of Brazil, Pedro II, was about to visit
Boston. There was to be a reception to him in Faneuil Hall,
and some schoolboy would have to perform in the recitation
of a passage of prose, which we may imagine came from
Daniel Webster. James Walsh of the Dwight School was
chosen for the honor. He spoke his piece with treble voice and
well-taught, perfectly unnatural gestures.

On this occasion, if not before, he must have become
conscious of his own self.

James—let those who knew him at that age, and them
only, be allowed to call him "Jimmie"—was an alert boy, and
very playful without being rough, and quick enough in his
lessons, and endowed with a ready tongue; wherefore his
parents—like all Irish parents, looking for some son to be set

apart for God's special service—decided that he was bent for the priesthood. His mother, resolutely ambitious in noble things, accepted the indications as certain. And so did the boy himself.

He wore the mark of promise without finding it a burden, for the obligations it involved lay far in the future. One Sunday a German Jesuit, Father Weise, spoke at his Sunday School in behalf of the orphans of China, and handed out cards to be filled with twelve cents for the ransoming of Chinese castaway infants. It was the work of the Association of the Holy Childhood that the Jesuit was carrying on. James Walsh, Junior, naturally took his card, and was no such bashful youngster that he did not go from door to door begging a cent a door. It gave him a feeling of importance. He remembered the feat in later life, but at the time it was no precocious deed of piety.

He also became a perfectly normal altar boy at the Church of The Immaculate Conception, jangling the bells at the right and wrong moments, near the towering, mysterious altar, and enjoying it.

His father was less a disciplinarian than his mother. When the family made its annual drive by carryall to Winthrop, young Timothy, the third child and third son, would every half hour ask for something to eat, and the father would never refuse to halt and buy something for the youngster.

The ambitious mother, on the other hand, was for spurring the children to something great, rather than for calming them with comforts. Andrew, known as Drew, was high-spirited and untractable. She was not sure what she could make of him. Timothy even from the cradle she destined to be an architect. James was to be a priest. She had a library at 14 Greenwich Park and encouraged him to read. She also had a piano and, since he had an ear for music, she taught him to play it. On Sunday evenings the house was given to hospitality, to the singing of folk melodies and popular songs, and the telling of stories, into all of which young James fitted as the musical son, who could play prodigiously the piano. To him the visitors turned their heads with compliments.

On November 10, 1877, the prodigy was confirmed by Boston's Boston-born Archbishop Williams. This man had seen a wondrous change in the Catholic Church in Boston since his birth in 1822 in the Irish colony down by Boston's present South Station. At that time there had been but three thousand Catholics in Boston, mostly Irish. Now there were over three thousand Catholic Walshes in the city, and a hundred and fifty thousand other Catholics. There were so many Walshes that young James not only took a Confirmation name, Anthony, but he inserted for general use the Anthony between his first name, James, and the last name, Walsh. It was time he was confirmed; there were troubles ahead.

In the following spring there came an Easter Sunday on which, according to the custom of the time, his father took his mother for a drive by horse and buggy. Mrs. Walsh was in feeble health, and the day was blustery and cold. She shivered, said not a word while she shivered, but forthwith fell sick of a cold, and died of pneumonia.

James Anthony Walsh now became aware of death, and

very soon became aware that there were ups and downs in human life, even in that of the well-established Walshes of Greenwich Park. Mr. Walsh was not receiving the profits from land speculation that he hoped for, and certain notes he had signed for his friends fell due for him to pay. He was straitened financially, and weakened by the loss of his wife and strengthener. He retired therefore from the brick house in Boston to a wooden house in Ellery Street (Number 103), Cambridge, just east of the buildings of Harvard College. He sold his two carriages and his horse, Bess.

The Walsh family were now seven in number, counting the bearded father. There was the first-born, Andrew, there was Timothy, and there was a still-younger brother, Joseph Berchmans; and there were two still-younger sisters, Margaret Beatrice and Elizabeth, after the last of whom had been named the horse, Bess. James Anthony had in this family to assume some of his mother's responsibilities, even at the age of twelve. He was competent and ambitious. He was somewhat like his mother.

As soon as he had finished grammar school, he went resolutely on to high school, choosing the Boston College High conducted by the Jesuits, next to the Church of The Immaculate Conception in Boston's South End. The mere going there cost some effort, for it was several miles off, as the bird flies, and he could not fly as a bird.

James Anthony was ambitious to excel at school; and, if he could not excel by being first in his studies, he could excel in extracurricular activities. Athletics was then a midday recreation rather than a field for distinction; and, even if it had been a field for distinction, he would not have excelled in it. His extracurricular activities were debating and journalism. The Jesuits made much of debate. There was a debating society named after the school's real founder, Father Fulton. Of it he became secretary. In 1883, his second year at the school, he won a debating prize of twenty-five dollars for having ably spoken *against* "Woman Suffrage"!

As a journalist, he took part in organizing *The Boston College Stylus,* a magazine which still continues. The position he held on the first editorial board was that of assistant business manager, which suggests that he was considered more sound of sense than brilliant of pen. Perhaps he was not pompous enough of pen to seem literary to the other boys or to himself, for schoolboys often mistake flourish for style.

Yet he continued to feel an attraction to the Muses, not only to Polyhymnia on his piano, but to Euterpe and Thalia, the ladies who presided over the theater. There was a cousin of his mother's, Mrs. Daniel Shea, who was now taking the place of his mother and encouraging his taste as his mother would have, had she lived. Mrs. Shea had a house in Boston and often on week ends young James, weary of commuting to Cambridge and of playing the mother to his brothers and sisters, would lodge under her roof and let himself be of her family and mothered by them. Mrs. Shea liked Shakespeare and liked the theater and liked taking her young cousin to see Edwin Booth, and liked, before and after the performances, as they drove from and back to the Shea doorstep, to recite the Shakespearian grandiloquence with laughter, and with frequent challenges to the young boy: "How does this go?

What's next?" He liked the private household pleasures of the Shea hearth and of his own hearth. He was not gregarious.

But now he was seventeen and the actuality of becoming a priest rose before him. He could catch a glimpse of what it meant to be a priest. There were great responsibilities ahead. Was he worthy of them? Not yet could he see into the inner secret of the priest's life. He felt an indistinct call, and at the same time a reluctance, for something in him held him back. Perhaps it was the great Opponent of Vocations picturing to him the priest's life as a chilling one. He envisaged it as a separation from the endearing pleasures such as these visits to the Sheas. The priesthood seemed aloof, its training cold, its life cold though heroic. He feared to lose his life's warmth. His life might not be meant to be a priest's life.

Not that he put it quite this way in his mind. He had not enough light in his mind to put it any distinct way. One day he felt this way, one day another. He was filled with doubts concerning his vocation. He was only seventeen.

There were at least not enough doubts in his mind to make him think of changing his mother's plans for him. He went on as if for the priesthood. He proceeded from Boston College High School to Boston College. It was an easy transition, for the college was contained in the same brick building as the school, and the three school years ran logically into the four years of the college. At the same time, for historical reasons, a step into the college amounted almost to a step toward the priesthood. Not until 1877 had Boston College given any lay degrees. It had begun as a pro-seminary; and, although the Jesuits were intent on changing its scope, the Catholic public were not fully conscious of its enlarged purpose. Therefore by entering the college department, in the autumn of 1884, he gave the impression to his relatives that he was taking a step toward the priesthood.

He went safely through his first term at the college, but in the second the condition of indecision began to numb his zeal and even to enfeeble his bodily health. Difficulties of minor importance exaggerated themselves in the cloudy atmosphere of his mind. His father was suffering new financial reverses. Was it fair for him to become the drain on his father's resources that he would be if he went on to a seminary? The toilsome journeys to and from Boston, which once had seemed as nothing, became interminable. They made him too tired to be of help in his own house, where help was needed. His brother Timothy had entered what people called "life": he was studying architecture in the architectural firm of Peabody and Stearns. James Anthony fell so sick of indecision that he quitted college and took up "bookkeeping."

During the summer of 1885, the difficulties began to evaporate. The financial situation of his family proved to be not so dire. The notes that his father had rashly signed were safely paid, and their payment left his father still so well off that he could retire from the liquor business (in response to a new attitude among Catholics, slightly puritan, that such a business was not respectable) and yet suffer no penury. Also the boy's health revived. Thus the premature plan to start supporting himself was cast aside as a somewhat feverish one. Instead he would continue his studies, not at Boston College,

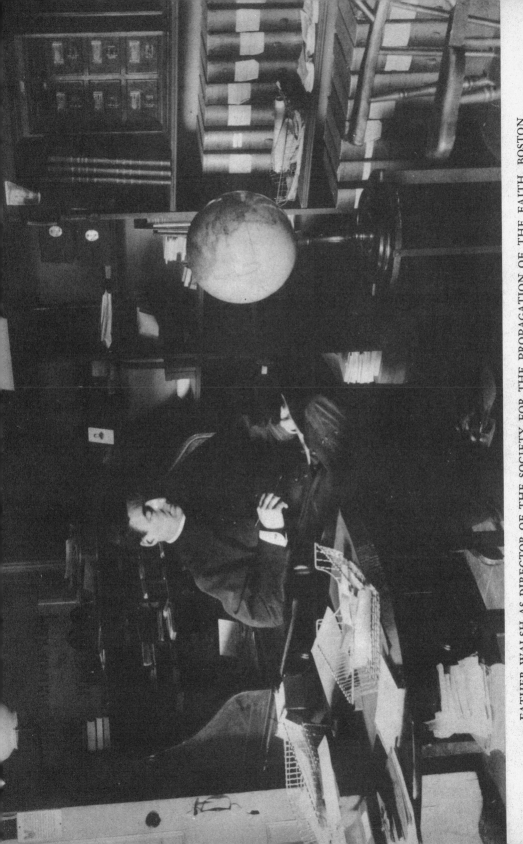

FATHER WALSH AS DIRECTOR OF THE SOCIETY FOR THE PROPAGATION OF THE FAITH, BOSTON

which was so far, but at Harvard College, whose buildings he could see if he craned his neck from his own veranda.

This transfer to Harvard was not a very decisive step. It scarcely made him a Harvard man, for he was entering Harvard only as a "special student," which meant that he was not a candidate for a degree, and that he had no intention of staying there very long. As a "special student," he would be outside the social life of the students. Also, he would be living at home, and thinking at home, and praying both at home and at the Catholic parish church across the yard, Saint Paul's, just as in previous years. Yet to some the step seemed to be a veering from his mother's plan, and a turning that would lead him from the priesthood, for Harvard was not considered a nursery for priestly vocations.

Harvard was more than a college of the liberal arts. It was at this time a temple, which not only Catholics, but Protestants of the old school, could shake their heads at. It stood as a challenge to the supernatural; as an exhibit of what human nature could do without calling on the help of grace. It respected a Creator, yet approached Him with a human respectability that saw no need of a redemption, and still less need of a priesthood. It worshiped an Unknown God, but with no altar, and no sacrifice, and it had no place for the "Cherub Contemplation" except in courses on fine arts. While it did not attack priests, its self-complacency rated them as supernumerary. Therefore it was held to be a place to lose rather than find a vocation.

Young James Walsh entered the Harvard Yard daily to

attend six courses. Four of them were language courses: Greek, Latin, English, and German. (French, in which he had excelled at Boston College, he dropped for the moment.) The two other courses were Mathematics and Chemistry. They were courses that made for a general education, and that did not point to any special career in life. They had nothing to do specifically with journalism. They were a continuation of his Boston College studies, and could be used as stepping-stones to a seminary if he chose to use them as such. In Latin he received a mark of 78, in Greek a little less; in German and English he received a passing mark. Six courses were too much: he neglected Mathematics and Chemistry.

Harvard in no way dazzled him into wondering if mankind needed priests. It did not dazzle him at all. In fact, in spite of the brilliance of this or that teacher, it struck him as a rather gray place, lacking a light which he very much needed. "I discovered," he said, "that I did not belong there."

Long before the academic year was over, he had decided to go where there was more light. It was not into journalism, much less into bookkeeping. It was not even back to Boston College. It was ahead to a place where men prepare for a special relationship with God. He announced to his family that he had definitely decided to become a priest.

"So that is what has been eating you up!" exclaimed Mrs. Shea.

The Seminarian

IN SEPTEMBER, 1886, James Anthony Walsh took a horsecar toward the setting sun, to the Brighton hills on which stood the seminary in which he would train for the priesthood.

"Six years before you will take a sleigh ride again!" mocked a cheerful friend.

The seminary belonged to the Archdiocese of Boston and overlooked both Boston City and Cambridge City. It was called the Seminary of Saint John, and was staffed by French Sulpician priests. It was but two years old, and was the first institution of its kind in the Protestant New England which had looked on the hatching of priests as the Devil's work.

So unused was Boston to the honor of possessing such a thing, that a *Dictionary of Boston,* published just at the time when James Anthony was entering this seminary, treated it as if it had been transported by a magician to Boston from remote ages and a remote country.

"The building is severe," said the *Dictionary* (beginning like a first paragraph of one of Sir Walter Scott's medieval romances), "and massive in its architecture, which is Norman in style. The walls are of agglomerate stone, quarried on the

17

spot and plainly treated, the trimmings being of brick, and the only relief to the general simplicity being the towers at the corners, which, with its great size and commanding position, give the edifice an air of castellated grandeur."

The *Dictionary* was not, any more than the vast majority of other books published in Boston, a Catholic publication. Its author was Edwin Munroe Bacon, and the writer of its preface was George E. Ellis, President of the Massachusetts Historical Society. Yet it strove to give the institution a place on the landscape, which it could do only by dwelling on its romantic mystery.

"Looking from the window of the library," it goes on, "with these relics of the past about one, and seeing black-robed priests pacing in meditation along the walks and under the trees, then glancing at the massive walls and turrets, and remembering that this is a nursery for the oldest Christian Faith, it is easy to recall the Middle Ages and their monasteries, and difficult to realize that within a few minutes' walk that prosaic institution, a horsecar, will bear one to the heart of modern Boston."

In truth the institution was not at all romantic and not at all medieval—for the semi-cloistered seminaries for priests dated but from the Council of Trent. Neither was it very foreign to the United States. At the outbreak of the French Revolution, Bishop Carroll had invited French Sulpicians to Baltimore. And since that day a great number of the Catholic parish priests of the United States had been formed by Sulpicians, either in this land or elsewhere. And though the Catholics had been but a tenth of the population, the history of a section of the country had been theirs, and the influence of Saint Sulpice had been important in that section. One can say even more than that: the Sulpicians had been woven into the westward expansion of our country. They were almost founders of Kentucky and of Detroit. They had a right to be considered affiliated even with New England, for Archbishop Williams and his predecessor, Archbishop Fitzpatrick, had both been Sulpician-trained.

Yet, for all that, the seminary showed itself strange to the nineteen-year-old individual, James Anthony Walsh of Ellery Street, Cambridge. He was not used to living, as he was going to have to live now, with seventy other young men in the same-colored clothes. He was not used to having a castle as his habitation. He had never, so far as I know, spent a night under a roof that did not belong to his father or a cousin of his. It was a decisive step to enter the portal of Saint John's Seminary. There were so many corridors, and seminarians and others who seemed to know where they were going in them.

For a few days—so his classmates say—he was a stander-apart. And some of the seminarians thought that his aloofness was due to the fact that he had been to Harvard, which had the name of fostering an offishness to Catholics. He was even looked on by some, possibly because of a real sensitiveness in regard to his personal attire, as a dandy, a fact which Father Walsh liked to recall with sly merriment thirty years later as an effective rejoinder to those, his former seminary companions, who had begun to chaff him for the over-shiny elbow of his cassock, and especially for his outmoded black receptacle of an 1898 hat.

But Monsignor Duggan of Hartford, his classmate, explains that very shortly his companionableness, if not his gregariousness—which he never possessed—became apparent. His fellow students "very soon discovered the deep faith, the keen intelligence, the unobtrusive piety, and the infinite humor of the young student." [1]

It was his humor which first found him his place. Monsignor Duggan calls it infinite, and it was pervasive, but never was it ubiquitous: otherwise it would never have been humor. In a worldly career his humor might have become cruel and sarcastic. Sensitive souls can use such a humor to protect themselves against a hostile environment, but in the seminary and in all his life it mingled a happy mischief with happier charity.

It was the custom of the seminarians to take their chief long recreation on Thursdays in the form of a walk behind their teacher, Father Chapon. Behind him they marched two by two, not in step, but semi-military in appearance. One day the procession met a counter-procession, a group of orphans captained by a Sister of Charity. The guileless, guileful tongue of James Anthony remarked to "Captain" Chapon how like they were to orphans guided by a kindly governess. After that the students were allowed to walk in less close formation.

Such a jest won him general gratitude.

Father Matthew Flaherty, an elder student at the seminary, remembers another quip of his which was very American but which won the smiles of the French Father Chapon, who was French enough to appreciate any real *ésprit*.

"I was asked the time," he recounted to Father Chapon,

"some years ago on Washington Street by a man, who thanked me cordially when I told him ten o'clock, casting a glance at my heirloom of a watch. But five minutes later, on feeling my pocket, I discovered the watch was not there. He had pickpocketed me."

"*Hélas!*" murmured the teacher.

"So I went with a friend to forget the loss by eating a happy dinner at the Parker House. I ordered ham and eggs. What was my astonishment, on looking up at the waiter, to discover that he was the pickpocket!"

"*Vraiment!*" ejaculated the priest.

"When he returned with the feast, I noticed his confusion. He was trembling in fright. He set the egg before me, and when I turned over the egg, do you know what I discovered?"

"The watch!" exclaimed the clairvoyant professor.

"No, ham!"

James Anthony made a place for himself in the community at the Brighton Seminary. He was the student who had the dry humor. He was the student who edited a student periodical which amused the other students. He was the student organist. But he made a special place for himself in the hearts of a few, among whom stood foremost James F. Stanton, a young man whose good looks Apollo would have been jealous of, had he lived in the days of Apollo. He might by Apollo have been changed into a tree—a magnolia or a flowering dogwood—as a punishment and a compliment. As it was, it was James Stanton's punishment to have ill health. Owing partly to his ill health, he was an omnivorous reader. He loved books. He delighted in the character of James Anthony, in his tastes and sensibilities, and in James Anthony as a wit found one with whom he could fence with his own wit.

James Anthony was in luck to find so congenial a spirit as James Stanton in his very own class at the seminary, but he also had the luck to knit other friendships, some of them with classmates who were not only dear to him, but who had abilities that stimulated him as a student and also aided him later in his life's work. One of them was the future Archbishop Dowling of St. Paul, with whom he could not compete as an intellectual, but for whose speculative mind he could have a real admiration. On the occasion of the Archbishop's death, James Anthony was to lament that this classmate of his had not written down enough of the "fine thoughts that he uttered." Charles F. Aiken was another student of marked intellectual ability, who later distinguished himself as a professor at the Catholic University. Peter F. O'Callaghan had an apostolic ardor akin to James Anthony's, and became influential as a missionary Paulist. Francis P. Havey became a noted educator of future priests, a Sulpician. Two others of his class became bishops: Bishop Guertin of Manchester, New Hampshire, and Bishop Anderson, Auxiliary of Boston. Last named but far from being last in loyalty, and one who was akin to him in journalistic ability, was the future editor of the Hartford *Catholic Transcript,* Monsignor Duggan.

But the purpose of the seminary was not to provide James Anthony Walsh with a homelike atmosphere and congenial companions, or to stimulate his private quips. It was to establish his mind in the orthodoxy of the Faith against the day when, outside of the seminary, he would have to lead himself and others amid doctrines erroneous and insidious. It was to develop in him an otherworldliness, and an heroic sense of being an apostle of Christ.

Seminaries in general had been established in order to separate candidates for the priesthood from a world grown blind and lax, in order that they might re-enter it and bring it a steady light. Boston was in many ways not lax, yet it needed the steady light. The Brighton Seminary was continuing the work of the seminaries, of preparing men for a peculiar service to God by withdrawing them temporarily from an alien world.

The Rector of the seminary was the Abbé Hogan. Born in Ireland, in County Clare, he had been taken to France in 1844, when he was fifteen, by an uncle of his who was a priest at Bordeaux. He had become utterly French. (A Frenchman said of him that his French was just a little too French.) He had become a French priest, a professor of theology at the central Seminary of Saint Sulpice, on *Plâce Saint Sulpice* in Paris. He had had French friends: Père Lacordaire, Montalembert, Ozanam. He had had French experiences; had learned of French Socialism before it came to America; had been imprisoned by the "Communards" and almost executed in 1871. Then in 1884 he had come to Brighton, a suburb of Boston, to the new seminary which Archbishop Williams was inaugurating.

The Abbé Hogan was no mere ordinary, competent, dutiful Sulpician: he was an extraordinary one, of towering personality. It was he who had general charge of the spiritual formation of all the students. To some of them he was spiritual adviser; to James Anthony Walsh he was such. He found a most ready and responsive and grateful disciple. Day by day James Anthony grew into an apostle according to the Sulpician mold.

One way in which the Abbé Hogan inculcated in his seminarians an understanding of what is general apostolicity was by acquainting them with the apostolicity of foreign missioners. He wished to show them that the days of the Twelve Apostles were not passed, nor were the days of Nero. The same Christian story of all the ages was still going on.

The Sulpicians are not themselves primarily foreign missioners. Recently they have adapted themselves to some pressing missionary work, and in the seventeenth century—the century of their origin—they had undertaken a mission to Montreal in Canada; or rather, they had founded Montreal as a Sulpician mission, and had sent their priests into the Mississippi Valley from Montreal. But in the main they have accepted as their sole work the training of diocesan clergy to be apostles at home. At this time they had no direct relation with the missions. Yet it happened that Abbé Hogan had had a special personal relation with missioners. Not far from the *Plâce Saint Sulpice* in Paris stood the Paris Foreign Mission Seminary on the corner of the *Rue du Bac* and the *Rue Babylone*. When the Abbé Hogan, in 1852, had been ordained at Notre Dame in Paris, with him had been ordained a student from that seminary, Théophane Vénard. This young priest had gone to Tonkin, in Indo-China, and there, in 1861, had suffered martyrdom.

It is safe to say that not many Americans, hearing the name

Tonkin now, could tell you where it is. Nor could they do much better, were they informed that it is one of the homelands of the Annamites. To the average Frenchman in 1860 it would have stood likewise for a locality very vague. Yet there were some French to whom Tonkin was very dearly known, and they were not few in number, although they were not the politically great in the land. They were the French contributors of money to foreign missions, who gave more than any other region of the Catholic world. They were the contributors of men to those missions, who gave more men than any other country—twice as many. To such, Tonkin was known not only as a mission field, but as *the* model mission field, not as large as others but the most fruitful. It was the land of martyrs, and also the land of promise and of harvest. In the late 1850's and early 1860's, over a hundred European priests were put to death in Tonkin, and over a hundred Annamite priests. As a result Tonkin abounded with conversions and native vocations, and even today it is an outstanding success of Catholic mission fields, with native priests outnumbering the European priests four to one.

In the very year that James Anthony entered the seminary, there was another persecution in Tonkin. The churches that were burned there numbered 163, and the massacred Catholics numbered 4,799. Abbé Hogan stood in awe of Tonkin. In that region—it is just south of China, on the seacoast of the peninsula of Indo-China—the apostolicity of the Church showed most gloriously.

So Abbé Hogan wished to acquaint his students with what was going on in Tonkin. And how better than by reading the letters which the man Théophane Vénard, with whom he had stood shoulder to shoulder, had written home to friend and relative during his suffering there?

I doubt if anyone could really know the priest, as he was to become, Father James Anthony Walsh, without knowing Père Théophane Vénard. The story of the French martyr entered into his blood at the Brighton Seminary. He found in him a companion dear to his heart, whose tender human affections called to his affections. James Stanton became his living comrade, but Théophane Vénard became his comrade almost as vivid. He made Vénard's acquaintance through the letters of the young man—he was only thirty-one when he died—which the Abbé Hogan read aloud.

Which letters they were, we cannot precisely know, but the letters were afterwards translated into English by Lady Herbert of Lea, and were amplified into a life by Father Walsh himself and published by him under the title of *A Modern Martyr*.

Like James Anthony Walsh of Cambridge, Théophane Vénard of Saint Loup in France had had a peculiar love for his family. Like him, he had broken home ties to go to a seminary.

"I had hardly come into the house (that is, the seminary)," he wrote his sister, Mélanie, "when I was met with affectionate greetings on all sides, and every kindness was showered on me. One hoisted up my trunk into my cell; another uncorded it; a third made my bed and showed me where my little establishment was to be; a fourth took me all over the house, introduced me to the Directors, and showed me the garden. In half an hour I felt as if I knew them all intimately. Oh, the good their welcome did to my poor, sad heart! There is nothing like the love and charity of this house, and the way they made me feel immediately at home." [2]

Then Théophane went to Tonkin, the land of almost-sure martyrdom, and he had from time to time to hide from the persecutions of the mandarins and the King of Tonkin, Tu-Duc.

"What do you think of our position, dear old friend?" he wrote to Abbé Paziot in 1860. "Three missioners, one of whom is a bishop, lying side by side, day and night, in a space about a yard and a half square. Our only light comes through three holes the size of a little finger, made in the mud wall, and these a poor woman is obliged to conceal by some fagots thrown outside. Under our feet is a brick cellar, constructed with great skill by one of our catechists; in this cellar are three bamboo tubes, cleverly contrived to have their openings to the fresh air on the borders of a neighboring lake. . . . We stayed with our poor old widow for three weeks, during which time I am afraid you would have been scandalized by our gaiety. When the three holes gave no more light, we had a little lamp, with a shade to prevent its tiny rays from penetrating outside through the chinks of our prison. One day we found ourselves surrounded, in fact completely blocked, by sentinels posted at every corner of the house, so that there was no possibility of passing from one house to another. An apostate who knew that we were in the village had betrayed our hiding place. Well, God defeated his plans." [3]

But God at last allowed Théophane to be captured.

"God in His mercy," he wrote, "has permitted me to fall into the hands of the wicked. On the Feast of Saint Andrew, I was put in a square cage and carried to the prefecture, whence I trace these few lines to you, with some difficulty, by the aid of a paint brush."

It was his bishop, Bishop Theurel, who wrote home the account of his execution:

"The executioner was a hideous hunchback, called Tûe, once a soldier, now a buffoon. He had already decapitated four of our priests on the 25th of March, 1860, and had begged to be allowed to perform the horrible office that he might have the martyr's clothes. He began by asking Father Vénard, as of an ordinary criminal, what he would give to be executed promptly and well. The answer he received was: *'The longer it lasts, the better it will be!'* Seeing that the missioner's clothes were new and clean, his whole anxiety was to get them without stains of blood. He therefore begged his victim to strip; and as this first invitation remained unheeded, he added, with barbarous ingenuity: 'You are to be *lan-tri';* that is, to have all the members cut off at the joints, and the trunk sawn into four parts. Our dear missioner, either because he believed the lie, or because he wished to experience more fully the humiliation of Our Savior, who before His crucifixion bore similar treatment, perhaps also because he was anxious to get rid of the importunities of this vile hunchback, took off all his clothes except his trousers. His elbows were then tightly tied behind his back, forcing him to hold up his head for the fatal stroke, and he was fastened to a stake badly fixed in the ground. In this position, at a given signal, Father

Vénard received the first stroke—but it was simply a trial blow on the part of the merciless executioner and did not enter the flesh deeply. The next stroke, more vigorously applied, cut the head nearly off, the stake and the victim falling together. Then the executioner, finding his sword blunt, took another, and hacked at the neck, while indignant murmurs rose from the crowd." [4]

Théophane Vénard could not remain remote to James Anthony, like one whom we read about in a book which may be fiction. He was not even history: he was news.

In the persecution of 1885 in Tonkin, another Frenchman had been killed, Gaspard Béchet. A little paper-covered book which told of his birth, life, torture, and death, came from France to the Brighton Seminary. James Anthony read it, and, while reading it, did something which few students reading such a story would have thought of doing. It was such a prosaic, down-to-the-ground thing to do. He noted that the address in France where the mother of Béchet lived was *17, Rue des Machabées, Lyon,* France. He copied down the address into his address book, as if he were going to make a call on that house. It was treating Béchet as if Béchet had lived very much in the world he was living in, and as if his home were not far from Ellery Street, Cambridge.

Foreign missioners became so much a part of the world of James Anthony that he began to do something about them. There was another professor at the seminary, Father André, nearer his age than the Abbé Hogan, and what he did for the missions he did with him. He and Father André united their thoughts. Father André had long thought of the missions, for as a young man he had nearly entered the seminary of the *Rue du Bac,* and had been deterred from so doing only because his advisers had pointed out that his remarkable talents as a teacher were needed elsewhere—at Saint Sulpice. He had a sister who was a Carmelite. He and James Anthony would pray for the missioners as prayed the Carmelites. He and James Anthony would send money to the missioners whom they admired.

They had no money themselves, but they would and could, working as journalists, collect alms. They edited a column called "Mission Notes" in a parish weekly edited by Father John C. O'Brien of the Sacred Heart Church in East Cambridge, *The Sacred Heart Review,* a magazine which by its quality circulated far out of the parish, even out of the diocese, even across to the Pacific Coast.

To make this column interesting was not difficult, for Father André was always receiving letters from missioners, and the letters were interesting by the strangeness of things they described, and by the strangeness of the heroic spirit in which they were written. Some of them were written as merely private letters.

"I am writing to you, my classmate," came one letter to Father André from a region of the Orient less fruitful in martyrs and in converts than Tonkin. "It is sixteen years since I left the seminary, with the fervor of youth and a strong desire to shed my blood for Christ. These sixteen years have passed in hard work with poor results. I have accomplished little and have come to the conclusion that nothing can be done in this district until some man's blood has been spilled;

(ABOVE) FATHER THOMAS F. PRICE, COFOUNDER OF
MARYKNOLL

(LEFT) FATHERS WALSH AND PRICE DURING THEIR
MEMORABLE MEETING IN MONTREAL, 1910

and I tell you in all sincerity, as friend to friend, coldly, far
from that fervor of the young apostle—that if tomorrow I
were called upon to meet death for Christ and souls, I should
be the happiest of men." [5]

This letter was not one to be published.

Other letters were more public. They were in the nature of
"relations" and indirectly were intended to stimulate the
giving of alms. From them James Anthony copied out excerpts
such as would catch the attention of the readers of *The Sacred
Heart Review*. He never lost sight of the nature of his audi-
ences. He made due use of the unusual, like a journalist. He
brought in pathos with passages from the letters of the director
of the Tokyo Leper Hospital. He brought in incongruity and
surprise with accounts of the Ursuline nuns living a frontier
life with intrepidity and versatility at Saint Peter's, Montana.
He was so busy with his column that he enlisted the help of
his sister Margaret, who shared his religious zeal as Mélanie,
Théophane's sister, had shared his.

The purpose of this column was primarily to awake Americans to what was going on in the foreign-mission field. As a
whole, the Catholics of the United States were unconscious
of missioners afar. Some of them still considered themselves
as a mission afar. Canonically the United States was still, at
Rome, listed as a missionary land, existing under the jurisdiction of the Sacred Congregation of Propaganda. The effort
of the Catholics had been to preserve their own faith in a
land of few priests, few churches, few schools, and few
orphanages. To think of so-called pagan lands in their own
dire hour of need seemed like unwarranted romanticism.

Yet Rome had early seen that an over-obsession with home needs might lead to an uncatholic provincialism. There were Catholic groups which were not indigent and were not in reality in a missionary condition at all. Pius IX in 1852 had urged the bishops of the United States even though under "Propaganda"—as we shall often entitle the Sacred Congregation—to collect funds for other bishops more in need of Propaganda's help. The bishops had echoed the exhortation, but very few funds had been collected for foreign lands.

Even as late as 1884, the Third Plenary Council in Baltimore had remarked that the negligence toward pagans had continued, and had remonstrated.

"In nearly all European countries," it said, "are foreign-mission colleges, and also associations of the faithful for the support of the missions by their contributions. Hitherto we have had to strain every nerve in order to carry on the missions of our country, and we were unable to take any important part in aiding the missions abroad. But we must beware lest our local burdens should make our zeal narrow and uncatholic. . . . We have therefore urged the establishment of the Society for the Propagation of the Faith in every parish in which it is not yet erected, and also a collection to be made yearly in all dioceses, for the foreign missions and the missions among our Indians and Negroes." [6]

Yet even the remonstrance remained a remonstrance.

Father André and James Anthony Walsh and Margaret Walsh found that, when the American Catholics really heard of the lives of missioners, they were not at all provincial or egotistic. Father André commented in amazement:

"It was wonderful to receive and read the letters that came to us from all quarters and in unexpected fashion. Sometimes they came from poor Irish servants who sent us their little savings and asked the unknown missioners to pray for them. Sometimes larger gifts came from mothers who wished to interest us in their children's future and in the success of the little ones' studies. Priests and seminarians added sincere congratulations to their offerings. We were happy and the future was promising." [7]

James Anthony Walsh found that his apostolic spirit was nourished, not expended, by the journalistic work that he was doing. The love of God was consuming him, and instead of becoming chill in his seminary atmosphere, he was becoming more ardent, more Christly human, and was in no way drying up the affections that he had feared to lose.

The years went by and he was approaching ordination. In December, 1890, he received the first of the major orders, the subdiaconate. His sense of vocation was a hundred times warmer and more articulate than it had been when, in 1886, he had told Mrs. Daniel Shea, "I have decided to be a priest." He now meditated with his pen:

"I have set aside the liberty of the world, but I have received thereby the glorious liberty of the children of God. I have taken upon me the angels' burden of intercession for the Church Militant, in return for which I am to receive countless benedictions and merits for souls. I have made what the world may call a sacrifice—which in reality is only the forerunner of joys innumerable, for what labor is sweeter than that of the faithful priest who spends himself for God and for the salvation of souls! My Beloved, then, has given all to me, and I in return have offered Him naught but a heart's affection until now too well divided. . . .

"Knit more strongly still this bond of love that unites my love to Thine, and may the union which it has been my happy lot to contract this day on earth be one day consummated in heaven—when I may see Thee face to face and live forever in the eternal bosom—O God—my Love. Amen."

Six months later, on June 26, 1891, he was raised to the diaconate.

Finally, on Friday morning, May 20, 1892, he became what he had so little understood when he had decided to become it—a priest of God. Archbishop Williams, who had confirmed him, now ordained him, in the Cathedral of the Holy Cross.

On the following morning, assisted by his teacher, Father André, whom he had assisted in editing "Mission Notes" in Father O'Brien's *Review,* he offered the Holy Sacrifice of the Mass at the Carmelite Convent in Roxbury. The Carmelites and he had been praying for foreign missioners.

Then on Sunday came his first Solemn High Mass, in his own parish church, Saint Paul's in Cambridge.

And after the Mass came the reception at his father's house in Ellery Street, at which he gave his blessing to his friends and relatives, both to those who prophesied great things for him, and to those who did not, both to those who were sure they had always been sure he would become a priest, and to those who remembered they had once had misgivings. One and all kneeled to him, kissing the new priest's hand.

"Six years before you take a sleigh ride again!" had said the mocking voice.

Six years were up, and he was not overjoyed that sleigh rides or any other childhood pleasures, from which he had been exiled, were now open to him once more.

What gave him more rejoicing was that after six years of preparation he could begin his life's work. Just what it would be, he could not exactly know. Some secular priests became professors like his teacher, Father André. Others grew up into shepherds of flocks, octogenarians with a whole town saying "Father" to them. Others became administrators, or great preachers, or hearers of confessions like the Curé d'Ars. Some became known; others did not. Some died in youth like flowers in unseasonable frost. Some became prelates, bishops with miters, or archbishops like Archbishop Williams who had ordained him. But whatever should be his particular task, he would take it up with the spirit which Théophane Vénard had shown in going to an almost-sure early death in Tonkin. Abbé Hogan had made him into an apostle.

The Parish Assistant

ON THE DAY after his first Solemn High Mass, Father James Anthony Walsh learned at least how his life work would begin. He had been assigned as assistant to Father Joseph H. Gallagher in Saint Patrick's Parish, Roxbury. He knew the region; in fact, he had celebrated his first Mass within its borders, in the Carmelite Convent. It was a mile or so southwest of his Boston College High School, in the thickly populated, wooden-builded hills of a district of Boston. At the time of his ordination, his father, proud of his son and wishing to have him enjoy a special advantage, had planned to send him to Europe for a glimpse of Europe's culture. But Archbishop Williams needed the new priest for immediate services; and so, after a breathing spell of two weeks, he presented himself to Father Gallagher, and was installed in Saint Patrick's rectory.

Saint Patrick's Parish was one in which the young priest would find it very hard to think of himself as a foreign missioner, or to perceive what analogy his life had with that of Père Théophane Vénard. The latter after his ordination had traveled to Antwerp and there boarded an American-built clipper, the *Phylotaxe,* bound for Singapore, which left Antwerp with the ceremonious salute of nine guns fired by the Belgian fortress. A trolley bell was all that saluted Father James Anthony's departure, and he did not have to pass by Singapore to arrive at his Tonkin—Roxbury.

It was difficult to imagine a parish more typical of the United States than that of Saint Patrick's. Possibly in some villages in the United States there were Catholic parishes which resembled village parishes in Europe. Possibly in Baltimore, or New Orleans, or Saint Louis, there were Catholic city parishes which resembled Catholic city parishes in Europe. But Saint Patrick's Parish, Roxbury, was a phenomenon peculiar to the United States, and especially to the northeast coast of the country—especially to Boston.

It swarmed with parishioners, many of whom were temporary. Nobody knew how many parishioners there were except that there were too many. Saint Patrick's Church itself was a new church, brick, Gothic—twelve years old—with an upper church and a lower—yet it was already outgrown. It was a parish which would soon have to be divided. Within the parish the census said that there were sixteen thousand souls.

The population of the parish was almost entirely of Irish stock. Most of them were poor, some of them had been maltreated in Ireland, and others in the United States, but they were happy. They were generally wage earners, but they had the hope of becoming capitalists. They were happy in their American opportunity. Most of them, if we count children, had been born in this country; but most of them, if we count only parents or grandparents, had been born in Ireland. Yet they were proud to be Americans and wanted to be more American than other Americans.

There was almost no social stratification among them. They were in a free-for-all for wealth and importance. There were few who entered professional pursuits, and still fewer who were bankers. The most prominent citizen among them was not a United States Senator, or State senator, or doctor, or manufacturer; he was the pugilist, John L. Sullivan! And John L. Sullivan was of the Catholic loyalty of most of the Irish.

The parish had come into being to meet the emergency of a sudden immigration. The priests in it had their difficulties, but they were not due to the anticlericalism of the parishioners. That in itself was an American as well as an Irish characteristic. The pastor, Father Gallagher, was a little man, uncommanding in appearance. A typical gesture of his was to feel the radiators in his edifices, with his finger tips, murmuring that coal was being wasted. Yet his prestige as a priest was prodigious. One day there was a parish gathering at which John L. Sullivan, not entirely himself, was present. Father Gallagher, a little over five feet high and thin as a broomstick, went up to him: "If you don't leave the hall here and now, I'll throw you out myself!" Out went the champion pugilist like a perfect lamb.

It could be said of the parish that its future was ahead of it, not behind it. It was scarcely intellectual, yet it had vigor. It was not decadent. In certain parts of Europe at this time, parishioners were divided by their own actions and in common parlance into two classes: practicing and non-practicing

Catholics. Those who walked regularly into Sunday Mass were practicing; those who were carried into a church for baptism and out of it for burial, and perhaps were lured in for their own wedding, were non-practicing. The faithful of Saint Patrick's were not all of the same virtue; but, generally speaking, they were one in attending Sunday Mass. They believed with the firmness of saints, even though they were not saints. They had a disdain for heresy and an incredulity toward social panaceas. Thus the work of the parish pastor and his assistants was not so much in seeking ways to establish contact with their flock, as in attending to the demands that their flock made on them. Father Gallagher had four assistants, and they were ever busy with celebrating Mass, going on sick calls, baptizing, conducting the Holy Name Society for the men and Our Lady's sodalities for women, and, last but not least in importance and labor, the hearing of confessions.

Saint Patrick's Church had by accident gained an extra-parochial function, that of hearing confessions of outsiders. This, with all due regard to the priests there, was not a tribute to their ability as spiritual directors. It was the trolley cars which were responsible. The church stood on the confluence of Blue Hill Avenue and Dudley Street, down each of which rattled and screeched trolley cars. Passengers going to and from work changed cars by the church, and seized the occasion of their wait to cleanse their consciences.

Surrounding the parishioners and mingling with them, was a population of fellow citizens who did not enter Catholic churches. Some of them entered no churches whatsoever. But they were all denominated Protestants. They were the vastly predominant part of the country's population, and they provided the setting for every Catholic parish. In Boston they were not so predominant numerically as elsewhere, but as a setting they were more rigid there than in some other places. They gave a character to the Catholic parish: they were another factor which made it active.

The Protestants who first came to Boston in Calvinistic days had been commercially active, but they had set faith above all things and had given no theological place to "good works." Now they had all but forgotten theological definitions of faith and of works, but they were all out for works. They worked individually to make money. But also they worked to elevate the community by education, and to lift it materially by social service. Catholics had to compete with this activity. Particularly they had to match naturalistic education with their supernaturally based education. And they had to meet more-or-less materialistic social service with Christian charity.

The parish was thus one with plenty being done, but also more to do. There was, for instance, no parochial grammar school for boys in the district, though there was for the girls a large grammar school and a high school, conducted by the Sisters of Charity of Halifax, which taught seven hundred pupils. There was nothing to correspond with the Protestant Y.M.C.A., though there was the great mercy of a Home for the Aged, conducted by the Little Sisters of the Poor. There was so much to be done, that Catholic vitality would have been submerged had it not been for the Blessed Eucharist of the altar of Saint Patrick's. And even with the Blessed Sacrament, and even with the prayers of the Carmelites, who were stationed so near the church, on their lordly named Mt. Pleasant Avenue, that the shadow of that mount cast an evening cool on the church, in the long summer days, the parish was in danger unless other things were done. Indeed, the Blessed Eucharist was calling for other things.

It was into such a parish that young Father James Anthony Walsh entered after six semi-cloistered years in a Sulpician seminary. It was like being thrown into the scurry and confusion of a battle straight overnight from the desk of a war college. The names of things no longer seemed to apply. Moreover, it was hard to see what was happening. His eyes were used to other, calmer sights. He was in a predicament like that of Plato's philosophers who, leaving their cave of generalities, found themselves blurred and blind in the particularities of the world. It would have been lamentable if he had drawn back, fainthearted, at the activity. It would have been tragic if he had gone all out for exterior activity.

There was no danger of his drawing back. Priests are not timorous. He was by disposition not timorous. But neither did he lose his balance, or become like the foolish oarsman who chucks form to the winds in the race's stress. He did not let himself be carried away by the purely external. He continued prayerful, and cherished the Holy Eucharist as the center of his life. It is significant that an aged parishioner, years afterwards, remembered him as the priest "made for sick calls." One day he went on a sick call to a dying woman, who had always had a great devotion to the Sacrament of the Altar, to Our Veiled Lord. It came over him as he attended her that she, growing blind, was on the point of at last seeing, and it made him feel, in comparison with her, in darkness. It was no original thought, but the power with which it took hold of him was unusual. The experience was ineffable, but something of it could be told. He could not help telling it. It became a poem, called "Only a Veil," which ran thus:

ONLY A VEIL

Only a veil between me and Thee,
Jesus, my Lord!
A veil of bread it appears to me,
Yet seemeth such, that I may not see
Jesus, my God.

Lift not the veil between me and Thee,
Jesus, my Lord!
These eyes of earth can never see
The glory of Thy Divinity,
Jesus, my God.

Keep then the veil between me and Thee,
Jesus, my Lord!
Some day 'twill fall when my soul is free
To gaze on Thee for eternity,
Jesus, my God.

It is in administering the sacraments that a priest finds himself nearest "the veil": his hand, as it were, goes through it and works beyond it.

At the same time Father Walsh took up tasks outside "the veil" with a supernatural zeal. He was the junior assistant of the parish, and his very name, Father Walsh, had been appropriated by a Father Thomas A. Walsh, a senior assistant. He became "Father James." But as Father James he was eager to

play his subordinate part. Several parochial tasks were assigned
to him specifically. He was given charge of Saint Patrick's
branch of the Holy Name Society—an •organization for men;
the Young Ladies' Sodality; the altar boys. And he had care
of the sanctuary, for which care he was well fitted, being by
nature given to neatness and having now directed the neatness
towards the things especially God's.

The Holy Name Society had originally been established in
the days of the Albigensian Crusade, two hundred years before
the discovery of America. It was not such a society as a priest
in the 1890's, in Ward 17 of Boston, would feel called upon to
revise. It was to be perpetuated. He did, however, give it a
custom new to the parish: it was from then on to have an
annual retreat lasting a week, which though it could not be
enclosed—all the men had their daily work—yet had its daily
devotions and instructions, morning and evening.

The women's sodalities were divided for two groups. The
married women went to the "real" Father Walsh—Father
Thomas A.—and Father James took over the unmarried
women. He was strict with them and asked them for a good
deal. They were to have weekly meetings, and attendance was
compulsory. But also he was gentle. If a sodalist was absent
from a meeting, she was liable to suspension; but, before
being suspended, she was always considerately followed up. In
his spiritual talks to them he showed that he expected from
them a real dedication to Our Lady. One of his sodalists with
a long memory has recalled: "He left one with a desire to
practice some special virtue during the week. He also urged
each of the members to have her own Bible, or at least a New

Testament, and to keep a crucifix on the wall of her room, low enough for her to kiss the feet of the Crucified Savior."

He gave great attention to the ceremonies of the sodality, and he chose the music for the hymns, which were played by Miss Anna Wetherell. This lady also acted as organist in the Carmelite chapel, accompanying there often the voice of an earnest, punctilious, high-collared convert—a Mr. Tuckerman, born of Calvinistic forbears, whose daughter had joined the Carmelite community as Sister Augustine and was to be their Mother Superior. High would go his voice as he grew older, and zealous and more zealous he waxed to be God's special soloist! But Miss Wetherell played the organ alone in the meeting place of the sodality, the lower church, and all the sodalists sang.

So definite was Father James's taste as to what tunes and what words should be sung that no existing hymnal suited him, or rather, suited what was his idea of the needs of the sodalists. Therefore, he made a selection of hymns and had them printed as the sodality's special hymnal. In that hymnal were various hymns with familiar words to which he had set new music, and among them was his own hymn—"Only a Veil"—to which he had given a wistful melody.

He gave himself, and more than gave himself, to the meetings of this sodality. At every weekly gathering, fifteen minutes before it began, he could be seen in an office near the Gospel side of the altar, waiting for members who might need advice or who might be coming to ask for special prayers. Only on one evening was he absent from this special rendezvous; that was the day when his sister Margaret—his

Mélanie—died, in 1895. Never did he treat these women as if they were to him a pious chore, to whom he had to do his duty, but with whom he was somewhat in haste to be through. It was his power of giving attention that attracted attention, and in spite of his strictness his sodality of the unmarried ladies prospered and held crowded meetings. It had over five hundred members.

When he took over the altar boys, he found that they had been well trained by a predecessor of his, Father George Patterson, who had a special sense of liturgical decorum. But altar boys would not always be altar boys. Some might become priests; others might fall among thieves. He looked intently at the boys to see what their future might be. And he encouraged those that needed encouraging. James Mellyn, who later became a Jesuit, was one of his altar boys and remembers how Father James showed confidence in him, gave him money to buy a little book, the ceremonial, and, perhaps more important, entrusted him with the errand of buying it, as if he were older than he was. Father James understood boys.

James Mellyn was not the only altar boy destined to become a priest. There was William Finn, who was to become founder and director of the Paulist Choir. There was young John Coveney, who was to be a Jesuit, and James Keyes and James McGovern, to be Jesuits with him. And there was Thomas J. Golding, a future secular priest; and Henry Murray, another. But Father James had a heart also for the boys who were not destined to be priests, who were quite obviously not so destined. They also were his.

It was for these latter that he established a society, the

Sanctuary Boys' Alumni. It was to make the boys forever
proud of having once been altar boys, no matter what troubles
and aberrations had beset them since. He summoned into it
boys who had been altar boys before he had arrived. Yearly
they held a reunion, and were not expected to look angelic or
very young in coming to it. It was his affability and humor
that attracted these boys and ex-boys. In 1900 Father James
wrote an account of how these reunions prospered:

"We began in a small way with the younger Alumni, in a
cheerless room in Roxbury, with a two-shilling lunch and
some weary and worn pieces of rope—called cigars.

"The music was of high order—so high that one of the
members cracked his voice in a high reach.

"Last year we made progress. We began to find the where-
abouts of former sanctuary boys, and in a large lower cabin
of the United States Hotel we heard for the first time the
memories of the day that went before we came. We saw the
bright manly faces, tried and true, of the once beardless and
'hairful' youths who had gained the sanctuary of heart, and
we realized that they still loved the beauty of God's house and
the place wherein His glory dwelleth."

Yet, in spite of all these organizations, a great part of the
work and play of the parishioners—especially the younger
ones—was going on without any Christian coloring. The
young were in danger of being piped into the materialistic
misery of becoming dancing mice, going feverishly nowhere.
The busy, well-meaning activity of the non-Catholics was beginning to lure them into its mill. Generous philanthropists
were ministering to them through various settlement houses

and other agencies which turned their eyes from their life's goal.

Of what he thought of mere this-world philanthropists, we know from his words at a speech at the Holy Ghost Hospital for Incurables, in Cambridge, when it was celebrating in 1900 its fourth anniversary:

"In these philanthropists, we often admire their activity in relieving the material wants of their fellow men, but we deplore and condemn the darkness of error in which, although strong in intellect and honest in judgment, they allow themselves to remain, unwilling to become as little children and with simple faith to bend their knees to the God of Truth. The lives of such men and women, so far as we can see them, are often well-ordered; their conduct right, according to the world's standards, but their influence is pernicious in the extreme—because it is insidious.

"They are sapping the life of faith in many. Consciously or unconsciously they are wolves in sheep's clothing. By kind acts and soft words, they are producing a fruitage similar to that which grows on the tree of Christ, and they present it that the world may admire it and be persuaded that the principle which produced it is life-giving and substantial. The artificial nature of this fruitage will yet manifest itself to all, but not until immeasurable havoc has been wrought and countless souls have withdrawn themselves from the Life of our life— and are lost to their God for eternity."

It was comparatively easy to say this, and it would also have been easy to let the matter rest there, and to do nothing about it. But Father Walsh did do something. He encouraged his young men and young women, for instance, to read, and to read as Catholics. Reading should be a Catholic activity, he taught, and not something divorced from the Church. To help them find books, he persuaded the City of Boston to establish a branch of its Public Library in the bookless region where he lived. The City was only too glad to help, and a library was established in what had once been the rectory, with the organist, Miss Anna Wetherell, as its librarian.

This left a still-unused upper floor in the former rectory. In it he organized a Catholic Young Men's Association. A hundred and fifty of the younger men joined it, and they attended classes there in English or elocution, or they studied to prepare themselves for Civil Service examinations. He invited Catholic laymen to lecture to them on general subjects; such men as Doctor Thomas Dwight, Professor of Anatomy at Harvard Medical School. In his own talks he did not sermonize, but he did entertain with stereopticon lectures. He knew how to approach their minds with not too "high-brow" instruction. He understood them. And he understood, too, that they needed athletic play. From the upper rooms of the old rectory were organized baseball teams and track teams.

And the young girls were not forgotten—even though, at Boston College High, he had argued against Woman Suffrage and won twenty-five dollars for doing it so well! He began a Catholic Young Women's Association, which in turn could use the same rooms. They received instruction in embroidery, cooking, dressmaking, millinery, stenography, music, Spanish, French, and "art." "Visit the art museums," he urged them, "and go to them as if they belonged to you. They do."

And young men liked to see young women. He united their activities in the presenting of plays, in the holding of dances, in singing together in a choral union, and in going on picnics. He established for young men and young women a periodical that they could both edit and both read, *The Catholic Associate*. This busy and engrossing life at Saint Patrick's seemed to him to be the kind of life that God was asking of him. Here was the work to which he would dedicate the short daylight of his earthly existence, "till the shadows lengthen" and God should present to him his "holy rest and peace at the last."

So excessively busy was he that at times he neared exhaustion, for he was never of adamantine health. He saved himself from real exhaustion, however, by being able to keep himself from being torn by emotions, either over-enthusiastic ones or over-depressing, and also by being able to take vacations and make the most of them. Once he went to French-speaking Canada as to a complete change. Some summers he visited New Hampshire, where there was a place called "The Knolls," the name of which, as well as the beauty of which, entered into his heart. But his happiest vacations were spent at Long Lake in the Adirondacks, whither he went with his boon companion, Father Stanton.

Both priests had a charming wit, but when together their wit was doubly charming. They cast light one upon the other, and sparkled. In the Adirondacks they won by their charm the very special esteem of Mr. and Mrs. Harry Harper, Quakers by religion, who, before they encountered Fathers Stanton and Walsh, had never spoken to a Catholic priest. Mr. and Mrs.

Harper had some wealth—they were of the publishing house of Harper—and they possessed a great deal of land on Long Lake, and they possessed generous hearts. They presented to the two priests a portion of the shores of Long Lake, where the Fathers built for themselves a camp, which annually rejuvenated them both. At it they acted as hosts to other Boston priests, their guests, whom they referred to as "fellow-members": Fathers Daniel Linehan, Thomas Golding, Frank Walsh, John Degan, James F. Kelly, and J. H. Courtney.

Father James had eyes which looked straight ahead of him. When God gave him a vacation, he took it. When God gave him work, he did it. He did not assume cares that belonged to God, nor did he become disquieted in regard to the tasks which were not his. Otherwise, with his sensitive nature, he could not have lived. This concentration of his kept him from thinking too much about the foreign missions, which at the seminary had filled his mind. They were not his affair.

Not that he closed his eyes to them, nor that he thought them unimportant. Of late, outward events had forced them and their importance on the minds of all thinking American Catholics. In 1898 was fought the Spanish-American War, which left the United States in control of the Philippines. This confronted the Catholics of the United States with the unhappy fact that their country had taken over at least one responsibility which it could not fulfill. There were no Catholic missioners in the United States who could take over the mission fields in those islands once manned by the Spanish friars. Why were the Catholics so unprepared? There were plenty of Protestant missionaries.

Furthermore, the Catholic hierarchy of the United States was bringing it home to the Catholic faithful that in elementary gratitude to God they should do more for Catholic missions in general. The American bishops had at last launched the Society for the Propagation of the Faith on a systematic collecting of alms. Father Joseph V. Tracy, formerly a professor in Baltimore, had been put in charge of this collecting agency in Boston. He had organized an *Academia* at Brighton Seminary to encourage a knowledge of, and enthusiasm for, foreign missions among the seminarians.

In every way the foreign missions appeared to Father James of Saint Patrick's as more important than ever. But God was not presenting him with a work which, so far as he could see, had anything to do with far-off things. He felt wedded to his parish organization in a lifelong wedlock. In 1900 Archbishop Williams suggested that he become an army chaplain, but he begged off by explaining how involved he was with the parish activities. For his societies he had contracted debts. Was it fair to pass those debts on to others?

In the summer of 1902, by way of change from his usual trip to the Adirondacks, he went to Europe with his friend, Father Stanton. It was a swift American tour: in two months they visited Morocco, Spain, Italy, Germany, France, England, and Ireland. Yet they saw deeply, none the less, and in seeing deeply Father James Anthony found his old enthusiasm for the missions blazing into new light.

He saw deeply especially in France, where in a most dramatic way he encountered both the spiritual beauty of France's Christian destiny and also her ugly repudiation of it. He knelt at the tomb of the recently deceased Abbé Hogan, whom he had so loved and admired, and who had introduced him to Théophane Vénard. Abbé Hogan, to his resentment, had been denied, by the persecuting French government, burial in the consecrated cemetery of the Sulpicians at Issy. He lay in the cemetery of Montparnasse, which, as Father James Anthony remarked, "had the name and stamp of paganism." This gave poignancy to his memory of the Abbé's spiritual generosity. As if the Abbé were still his guide, he visited the *Missions Étrangères*—the Paris Mission Society—on the *Rue du Bac*. And the other French priest, his special friend, Father André, came up from Avignon to meet him, and continued to treat him as if they were both still one in the ardor of long ago, collecting money for the missions through Father O'Brien's *Review*.

His trip to Europe did revive in him a missionary enthusiasm half-forgotten. When he returned to Boston, he gave a series of three lectures, with stereopticon slides, under the auspices of his Catholic Young Men's Association, in which he not only regaled them with all that he had seen of the picturesque on his travels, but also stirred them with accounts of the mission societies which he had visited: the one at Paris; Cardinal Vaughan's Mill Hill in England; and the Milan Foreign Mission Society. He mentioned Théophane Vénard and Tonkin. But it was not to turn his hearers into missioners, or to divert his own attention from his Roxbury duties: it was to make them and his own self more apostolic at home.

One day he heard that representatives of the S. P. F.—as we shall often call the lengthily named Society for the

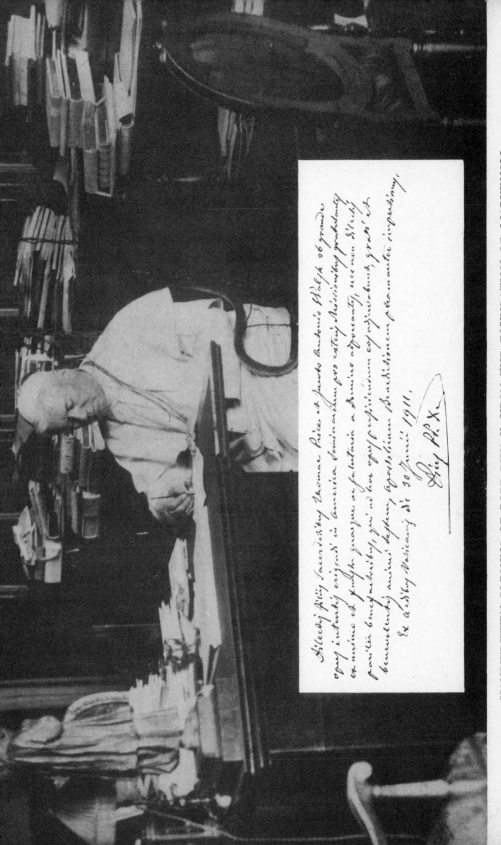

HANDWRITTEN BLESSING OF POPE PIUS X UPON THE FOUNDATION OF MARYKNOLL

Propagation of the Faith—were to be chosen for every parish, and he feared that Father Tracy might choose him as the appropriate representative of the S. P. F. in Saint Patrick's Parish. He had a dread that his parish lifework might be interrupted. Then the choice was made known. It was indeed Father Walsh who was chosen, but it was Father Thomas A. Walsh. He laughed at his own egotism: he had forgotten that God had quite a number of Father Walshes. He was behaving like one with a guilty conscience.

But a trap was being laid for him by God. Father Tracy found that his double work—he was also a teacher at the diocesan seminary—was too much for his health, and he offered his resignation as Director of the S. P. F. The National Director, Father Joseph Freri, at Baltimore, was trying to think of a new Director for the Boston Archdiocese, and he knew nothing of the Boston priests. He had a secretary, however, a layman named Moses Hale Douglas, who did.

Douglas was a convert. He had been converted while studying at the Protestant Union Seminary, and one influence which had drawn him to his conversion was the example of his cousin, Langdon Ward. The latter had once been an Episcopal minister, assistant at Trinity Church, Boston, and had become a Catholic, and then had taken a position at the Boston Public Library, in which position he had become a friend of Father James Anthony Walsh of Saint Patrick's, who knew about books. Through Langdon Ward, Douglas also had made the acquaintance of Father Walsh. He knew nothing about the seminary experience of this Father Walsh, who had dreamed so much of the missions, but he was quite sure that he was a man and priest of rare distinction. "Choose Father Walsh."

Father Walsh knew nothing of Douglas's conversation with Father Freri, and did not know Father Freri. But the net was closing about him. Father Freri arrived in Boston to talk with Archbishop Williams.

One March day in 1903, Father James saw in the Boston *Pilot* that Doctor Joseph Tracy was to be assigned to a parish because of ill health. No longer was he to direct the S. P. F. Once again the thought leaped through Father James's mind: "I am going to be enlisted in foreign-mission work. I am going to be the next Director of the Propagation of the Faith in the diocese." Then he remembered his former bit of egotism, when he had imagined that he was slated to be parish director. "I smiled," he recorded later, "and wondered why that thought should have come to me at all, and so strongly. Then I put it out of my mind."

This day was an important one for Father Walsh. He remembered it with strange vividness years later, and even more minutely he remembered the next day.

"The following morning, Saturday, I was going downtown on some business, but I was held up by an old lady who had a long story to tell; and, by the time I got through with her, it was too late to go downtown. So I went into the garden to say some office.

"By this time I had quite forgotten about the Propagation of the Faith; but, as I happened to look up, I saw a man with a beard go to the front door. As the maid opened it, I said to myself, 'That is the Central Director of the Propagation of the Faith, and he has come to ask me to take the position.'

"About two minutes later the maid appeared to call me. It was as I thought, and Father Freri, after a brief greeting, said that he had come from Baltimore to see the Archbishop and had come here to ask if I would succeed Doctor Tracy. I asked how much time he wished for an answer, and he told me that he was anxious to get back to Baltimore as soon as he could. I promised a reply in twenty-four hours, and he left.

"I could see no reason why I should not take that position; and, when I found that the Archbishop had signified his willingness, I got in touch with Father Freri and accepted the position.

"The following Monday morning I was at the office of the Propagation of the Faith. When I took that position, I said to myself very positively, 'I am going to stay at this work in some form or other for the rest of my life!' " [8]

As the Judean prophet, Habacuc of old, had been lifted by an angel, who grasped him by the hair of his head, and had been transported by that angel from Palestine to the world center of those days, Babylon, so Father James Anthony found himself, through no volition of his own, transported from parish work in Saint Patrick's Church, Roxbury, to work with the S. P. F. at Boston's Cathedral of the Holy Cross, in the South End.

"I have not seen Babylon!" remonstrated Habacuc with the angel just before the angel set hand to the crest of his head.

"Why me?" murmured Father James.

But Father James had arrived, and he had only to open his eyes. And he did open his eyes.

Director of the S.P.F.

"Good MORNING, Father," said Miss Eunice Divver, as the new Director entered the office of the S.P.F. at 62 Union Park Street.

Miss Divver had been secretary to Doctor Tracy. She knew where the files were, and what was in them. She knew what letters had last been written, and what were to be written. She would be invaluable. It was ten years or more since Father Walsh had been corresponding with missioners and collecting money for missioners. His sister Margaret had helped him then.

The office was not large or luxurious. It was a single room, up one flight, in a two-story, wooden, unimproved building, which contained Mrs. Farrell's Laundry in the other second-story room, and the City of Boston's Branch Library on the bottom floor. In the office there was a spacious desk for the Director, with flat wire baskets piled with correspondence—that morning's—of which the postmarks were China, Japan, the Malay Peninsula, Africa, and—Lowell, Massachusetts. There were bookcases ranged against the walls. There was a framed certificate of the Boston Branch of the S.P.F. hanging

56

on the wall. There were several spears from the South Sea Islands on another wall. There was a statue of Saint Francis Xavier on the bookcase. There was a globe of the world, the size of a child's balloon, on a small table. There was a passage for one's feet in going from table to table. It was as crowded as his friend Father Stanton's room was ever crowded with books—books which stood in cliffs and pinnacles here and there even on the floor—but it was in better order. There was a desk for Miss Divver and her clacking typewriting machine.

Father James looked out the window. Full in his face stood the flank of the Cathedral of the Holy Cross, of granite rusty and gray. Its tower was his neighbor. A few yards down to the right ran Washington Street, the old original road from Boston peninsula along Boston's isthmus—"the Neck"—to Roxbury. It was cobblestoned, and from its pave rang the incessant music of horses' hoofs and clangorous-wheeled drays. It smelled of leather, wool, and saloons. Near to it lay, not China, but Boston's Chinatown. Seagulls from Boston Harbor's South Cove drifted over his head. He was like a bird in a nest. He called his office "The Rookery."

He began his work, and what he began in the morning he finished before night. He never left a disordered desk; it was against his principles so to do, and against his liking. Disorder meant a waste of time. Never in a hurry, he always counted time precious. He guarded it, partitioning it, doing one thing at a time, thoroughly, with complete attention.

He inherited his task from Father Tracy, who had done it well, with a minimum of space, a minimum of time—for he had been a professor of Sacred Scripture at the seminary—

and less than a minimum of physical strength. It had been a task indirectly handed on to Father Tracy from a French lady, Mademoiselle Pauline Jaricot, who in 1819 had decided to support foreign missioners by asking her friends to find ten other friends who would be willing to give one cent a week to foreign missions. In times past kings—especially the kings of Portugal and Spain—had supported foreign missions. Then Rome in the seventeenth century, a bit suspicious of the secular ambitions of kings, had established the Sacred Congregation of Propaganda on the *Piazza di Spagna,* and had endowed it with landed wealth, from which some missioners could be supported. But the French Revolution had swept away such endowments. Only the multitudinous poor could now support the missions with multitudinous mites. Pauline Jaricot started a system of collecting which became the Society for the Propagation of the Faith, with headquarters in Lyons, France. Father Tracy was continuing her work of cent collecting at the diocesan branch of the Society in Boston, Massachusetts. He had been at it for six years.

The collecting of cents in Boston was not done by going from individual to individual. It was done rather by going from parish to parish. The goal was to establish parish branches of the Society in as many parishes as possible, which branches should be made up of various classes of members: ordinary, who gave sixty cents a year, and special, who gave six dollars, and all of whom were expected to say one "Our Father" and one "Hail Mary" and one "Saint Francis Xavier, pray for us," daily. In some of the parishes there were regularly appointed priests who acted as parochial directors, but in such parishes, and also in others where there were no parochial directors, it was the usual method to group the members into groups of ten under a promoter who would collect their offerings and circulate among them the *Annals of the Propagation of the Faith,* which was sent out every two months. The offerings were then turned over by the promoter to the parochial director, if there was one, or directly to the Diocesan Director.

In order to enlarge the Society's membership, it was therefore necessary for the Diocesan Director to stimulate the interest of the promoters. He had to have some personal magnetism and some contagious enthusiasm. But in order to have access to the promoters, he had first to gain the cooperation of the parish pastors, which took tact. Once he had the cooperation of the pastor, he could face the parishioners at the various Sunday Masses and, speaking to them, awaken them to becoming members of the S. P. F.—and even promoters of it.

Outside of this regular channel, it was possible for the Director to appeal to rich individuals for gifts. And occasionally, usually from a priest, a testamentary bequest might arrive. But it was the regular income that was most necessary, and, in order to be regular, it had to come from as many as possible, and from as many parishes as possible.

Before Father Tracy had taken up the Directorship in Boston, various individual priests had been collecting money for the S. P. F. From 1854 to 1884, Boston Catholics regularly sent a thousand dollars a year to Lyons, one third of which returned to the United States, for the United States was still a missionary country. After 1884—after exhortations from the American bishops—the collections at Boston tripled. When Father Tracy took charge, this tripled income quintupled, and by 1901 it was twenty-five thousand a year. Father Tracy was an heroic little man, with health so frail that he had never been able to pass a single year complete as a student at Brighton Seminary, and with an intelligence so keen that, by the time he had graduated, he was competent to be a teacher. When he spoke on Sunday, at the six morning Masses of a great, crowded, city church, he did not speak in vain. He was the bird, the heroic early bird, but now he could not go on being early and late.

The first thing Father James did, after he had cleared his desk daily for a few weeks, and preached a few foreign-mission sermons, was to go abroad. It was not in order to recruit his health, or to pass the time. He treasured time. It was to become more familiar in the concrete with the foreign-mission situation. Winning the favor of pastors so that he could collect money in their often debt-ridden parishes required tact. The tact that could establish contact with the pastors had to appeal to their heads as well as to their hearts. A mere gracious manner on the part of Father James might find for him friends but not cooperators, for they set up a defense against vague sentimentalism when it came to the question of finances.

All pastors everywhere and in every age—so I suppose—need money, but these pastors in the Boston Archdiocese needed it for things elemental. Even where they had large churches and parochial schools already established, they had in no sense arrived at their necessary material equipment.

They had debts and many concrete needs, and the resources of their generally not-rich parishioners had to be guarded and not wasted. Father Walsh from his own parish experience understood their attitude. Thirty years later Father James was to say of them: "There were priests—good earnest men—who felt that a dollar sent abroad would weaken just so much the Church at home, and that it was nothing short of foolishness to encourage vocations to a foreign field." [9]

He was not yet asking them for vocations, but he was asking them for money, and to have that he had to break down a resistance that existed in their heads. First of all he had to detach the foreign missions from a vague romanticism. To do that, he had to present to their eyes foreign missioners individually, whom they could look at and not think of as storybook characters. He had to prove to them that funds to the S. P. F. were going really somewhere. Only by possessing himself of a clear acquaintance with the missioners being sent out from Europe could he hope to be able to speak of missions with a prosaic clarity to the pastors.

Visiting Paris once again, he made inquiries of Father Delpech, the Superior of the foreign-mission seminary in the *Rue du Bac,* such inquiries as before might have seemed officious inquisitiveness. This Father had been a classmate of Théophane Vénard. Like a reporter, Father Walsh questioned Father Delpech concerning Théophane. Did he have any family left? Yes, a brother, Eusebius, a priest. He had not time to visit Père Eusebius now, not on this trip, but some day he would. "But may I see your museum, with its relics of the martyrs?"

He learned concerning the situation in China, learned who was who among the missioners, learned what were the greatest needs of missioners, and how they were trained. And how would the French missions fare under the growing governmental persecution of all that was Christian in France? And how about the Italians, the Spaniards, and the Hollanders, who were now becoming for numbers the wonders of the mission field? And how about the English? England's Mill Hill—the foundation of Cardinal Vaughan—was recruiting in Holland as well as in England, and it had a home in the Tyrol. He visited Mill Hill, and knit a friendship with its Superior, Father Henry.

Father James returned to America with his mind stored like a journalist's with intimate details, intent on making foreign missions a home affair. He did not have to rely on vague appeals for suffering lepers, which always aroused momentary emotion, or for abandoned Chinese babies. He could distinguish himself from a "foreign-mission maniac"— the phrase is his. He could be hardheaded.

Did the debt-ridden pastors realize that in giving money to the S. P. F. they were paying off a debt—part of a national Catholic debt? Had it not been for support from Europe— from the S. P. F. and the German-Austrian Leopoldine Society —there could scarcely have been any church buildings or any hierarchy in the United States. And Boston had her own debt, which, although it had literally in dollars and cents been paid, had not been fully acquitted with gratitude. In Bishop Fenwick's time Boston, as a "romantic" mission to Europe, had received four thousand immediately needed dollars from the S. P. F.

After that he could even sermonize. The general spirituality of the parishes in Boston would be helped by an interest in the heroic apostolicity of the Church. And had not Christ bade his disciples to go forth and "teach all nations"? Somebody had to go. If Boston could not go, it could help support those somebodies who could go.

And coming down to figures, was he really asking for very much? The pastors were merely being asked for crumbs. The motto of the S. P. F. was only this: "Gather up the fragments that remain, lest they be lost." (*John vi, 12*)

Father James continued Father Tracy's work with more health and more time than Father Tracy had been able to devote. He was collecting from over a hundred and forty parishes in the archdiocese, and from seven New England dioceses outside Boston, where there were as yet no Diocesan Directors. Eight parishes began to give over a thousand dollars a year. Those two which gave most were parishes conducted by French missionary orders: that of Saint Joseph's in Lowell, of the Oblates of Mary Immaculate; and that of *Notre Dame des Victoires* in Boston, of the Marist Fathers. Next to them his own parish of the Holy Cross Cathedral gave the greatest amount. The Immaculate Conception Parish in Salem —of which the pastor was Father T. J. Murphy, and of which the parish director was his friend and companion at Long Lake, Father J. H. Courtney—came fourth. Among the eight which gave over a thousand was that of Father John O'Brien, the Sacred Heart Parish of East Cambridge, with which

Father James had been associated in writing for *The Sacred Heart Review.*

There were gifts, too, and many of them were very touching, for they came from the not-rich. One day Miss Divver was sitting in her office at 62 Union Park Street. By then the lower floor of the building had been vacated by the branch of Boston's Public Library, and she had a large office, and one to herself, one which Father James, after his visit to the museum at the *Rue du Bac,* had transformed into a museum. It was a summer day and the half-open street door was flung open fully as if by a wind, and in stumbled an inhabitant of the district, which was not one of elegance. He was a man, and his face was red, and she feared he had been taking, in face of the enervating heat, some over-exhilarating refreshment.

She had some money—contributions to the S. P. F.—in her desk drawer. In her dread of what might happen, she cast an eye, warrior-like, at a spear from the Solomon Islands, hanging on her wall. Could she seize it, brandish it, and save the castle? The ill-dressed man lurched, smote the table with the palm of his hand—and, departing, left behind two twenty-dollar bills.

On other days surprises came in a different sense. One spring day a lady arrived in silk and in charm. She danced up the stairs. Outside there were a coachman and a shiny carriage, and the horses pirouetted. Father James in his "rookery" sensed great things. But after she had left, Father James descended with a smile more rueful and amused than joyful. "She asked me to bless her ring."

But the happy surprises were the more frequent. In the year

1904 he collected thirty-seven thousand dollars in membership fees and gifts, which was over a fourth of what the entire Catholic United States contributed and more than any other diocese in Christendom. And this sum did not include forty-five thousand dollars which came in testamentary bequests.

This was very handsome and brought him various congratulations, such as that from the Paulist, Father Walter Elliot:

"Only yesterday I read the good news that Boston heads all Catholic Christendom in contributing to the propagation of our Holy Faith. Thanks be to God! And many sincere congratulations to you, who are the chief cause under God, for so favorable a result. And I know that you will not 'let well enough alone'; but will set all so magnificent an example of zeal for souls united to fine organizing methods, as soon to place the Church in America where she ought to be—in the forefront of all Catholic missionary enterprise among the heathen."

This letter gave to Father James the courage to write a letter, himself, to Archbishop P. J. Ryan of Philadelphia, urging him to establish a branch of the S. P. F. in Philadelphia.

"Under separate cover I am sending a copy of the Boston Diocesan Report of the Society for the Propagation of the Faith. I do this because I believe that it will interest one of your breadth of thought and action to know what can be done by this systematic gathering of the crumbs. I also feel that this report will illustrate the possibility of helpfulness to our home missions.

"Today the S. P. F. receives from the United States about

$100,000, of which amount at least 25% is apportioned to the U. S. missions. If the S. P. F. were widely organized here, I believe that $1,000,000 could be secured annually, and if 30% of this sum would be devoted to our home needs, we could have $300,000 at our disposal for work among Negroes and Indians, for poor dioceses and perhaps for the non-Catholic mission work. Besides, our people could be thus united in one great missionary effort, a practical exemplification of the Communion of Saints.

"I have much to say on all of this, but I do not wish to take up your time."

He urged the same on Archbishop Farley of New York by word of mouth, and tactfully suggested, as a proper organizing priest to become its Director, Father John Joseph Dunn, curate of the Church of Saint John the Evangelist in New York City. The Archbishop took the suggestion, and appointed this Father Dunn as Diocesan Director, and thus began an affectionate collaboration between Fathers Dunn and Walsh which was ever to increase with the years. But before he made the appointment, he asked Father Walsh to sound out the young curate; and Father Walsh, in sounding him out, and coming on him when he was busy with a catechism class, received from him, before he gave his assent, a remark made with a quick turn of the head: "The S. P. F.—and what is that?"

If a zealous young priest, alert and apostolic, could ask such a question, even half in earnest, what could be expected of the rank and file of Catholics? "The S. P. F.! What is that?"

Father James was thus not being deceived by his success. It

was a very comparative one. For all the jubilation of Father Elliot, and his own agreeable self-congratulation at the sums for the S. P. F. being collected in Boston, not in Boston or anywhere else in the United States did there exist a situation which could make anyone interested in missions optimistic. The fact of it was that the Catholics of the United States were not doing what they should be doing.

France, though suffering from a persecution by an anti-clerical government, in which the Church in France had lost its property, was giving five times as much as the United States. The Protestant Episcopal Church in the United States, numerically unimportant although conspicuously rich, was giving seven times as much to its foreign missions. And the reason for the Catholic shortcoming was obvious. It was not that Catholics' hearts were not generous, but that their heads were not conscious of foreign missions. American Catholics were, to use a phrase of Langdon Ward's, more conscious of "the fold" than of "the field."

And how could they help being that way? The Protestant Episcopalians of the United States had missionaries in the foreign field, and that fact helped to make the Episcopalians conscious of those fields. The Catholics of France did not have to make an effort to remember China and Indo-China and Japan, where their relatives were laboring. The Catholics in the United States had no brothers and sisters in the missions. It was sheer love of God, or in some cases an impersonal sense of duty, that led the Boston Catholics to give what they did. They were giving all that could be expected of them so long as they had no missioners in the field, but not one tenth of what they would be giving if they had.

One way to awaken the imagination of American Catholics to foreign missions was to show them American missioners who were working within the United States, in regions often as difficult as any in the Orient—among Red Indians, for instance—and then to transpose their interest in those missioners to the European missioners in Asia or Africa.

Right next to the Boston office of the S. P. F. lay Boston's Chinatown. China was huge. Statisticians liked to play with the figures of its population. It had more inhabitants than North America, South America, Africa, and Oceania, taken together. "If the population should join hands, singing in an unbroken line, they would reach ten times around the world." [10] Boston's Chinatown contained fewer souls than crowded into a railroad train some summer afternoon in the South Station. But no matter, it was a population large enough to begin on. And there was a Father Walter J. Brown who was working with these Chinese. He had a catechism class, and in 1903 had baptized his first convert, Joe Fie Ark, who immediately became, after laundry hours, a frequent visitor at Father James's office. Father James often met these catechumens, and even sat with them to have his photograph taken. Catholics should know of such things. It would turn their attention from the fold to the field and warm them into a disposition more apostolic.

But how many Boston Catholics gave two thoughts to Boston's Chinatown? The Catholics of the United States were largely immigrants who had entered into a region which they felt to be hostile to their religion, and which was, all in all, hostile, and against which they were intent on defending

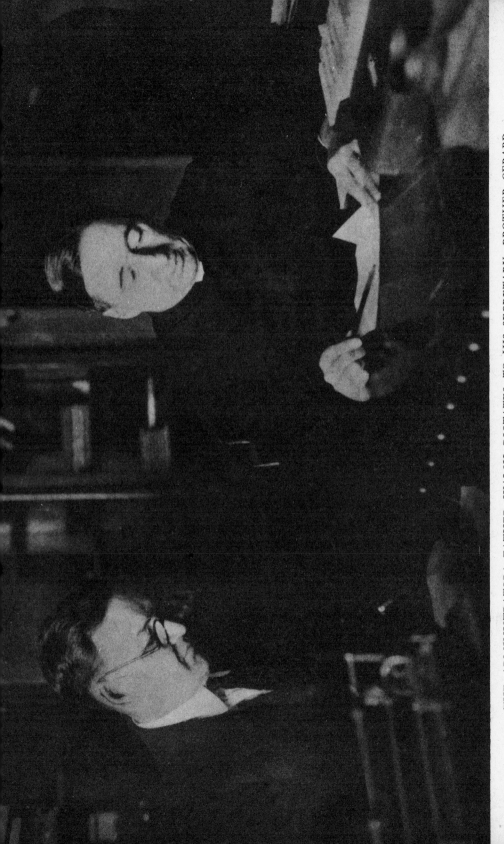

THE ADMINISTRATOR: FATHER WALSH DICTATES TO HIS SECRETARY, BROTHER GERARD

themselves. Too often they had too little zeal and confidence in bringing their gift from God to their fellow citizens. Home missions could not awaken their imaginations to foreign missions, for the reason that home missions had themselves not entered into the imagination of American Catholics.

It came over Father James that American Catholics could not be awakened to their apostolic obligation until they first caught sight of their obligation to the whole world. How to give them that sight was a question. Certainly it would not be well to rail at Catholics for their shortcomings. Human nature does not respond well to mere scolding. It is so easy and so futile for one man to find fault with others.

It was at a meeting of the Missionary Union—an American organization chiefly occupied with the supporting of missions to isolated Catholics in the United States—in Washington, D. C., in 1904, that Father James first publicly presented his view that the whole world must be envisaged by American Catholics before they could be awake to any part of it. He delivered before the congress a speech which began in measured terms:

"While conscious of the need of priests in most parts of our country, I believe that to send some of our young men and women to more remote districts would stimulate the vocations for home needs, and especially for the more remote missions of the United States."

But soon the speech by careful, logical steps began to talk about the whole world, about the relation of a priest like himself to the whole world:

"The true priest lives his short life for the salvation of his fellow creatures. Every sincere Christian longs for the day when the Kingdom of his Savior shall rule all men's hearts. What we priests and laymen can do by effort and prayer to win the world to Christ, this we should do, so that the altars may be more numerous on the earth than the stars in the heavens; that multitudes in every land may be nourished with the Bread of Life—the Body of Christ; that this earth may be deluged in the Precious Blood of the Lamb—a ruby earth glistening like a radiant jewel under the sunlight of the glorious Cross of Him who died on it, *not for you or me alone, but for every child of man."*

To transform the image of the whole world into a small jewel in the mind's eye requires a certain heat in the soul, such a heat as in a different order of things reduces a pile of slag to a small diamond. In composing the speech Father James had felt himself touched by such a heat; it was not a borrowed figure of speech that he was using. And in delivering it he had felt himself further welded by a flame. He related in after years to Monsignor Duggan how, when he was speaking these words, a sudden clarification had taken place in his mind, which experience the Monsignor has himself related to us in the following words:

"Suddenly a thought came to him, a thought which could be translated into words like these: 'Here is your life's work. Go on, and I will be with you.' He recognized the message as coming from on high. Never did he forget it, and never did he falter during the dark days that followed." [11]

While Father James was speaking these words at the congress, there sat looking at him a battle-scarred missioner of the mission land of the United States, Father Price of North Carolina. Some men in their minds see the whole first, and then the parts. Others put part and part together and suddenly catch sight of the whole. I suspect that Father Price was of this second kind. I doubt if he came to the Congress of the Missionary Union with the world in his mind's eye. He saw Our Lord and Our Lady against the background of his own dear land of North Carolina, where there were fewer Catholics in proportion to the population than there were in China, and where still, as I write, there is a single parish as large as Ireland with only fifteen Catholic families in it. His heart was tied to North Carolina. Yet as he listened to Father James, his North Carolina stood for the world.

Many American Catholics, living not far from North Carolina, scarcely gave that State—his State—a thought. Here was a Catholic feeling in regard to the whole world as he felt in regard to North Carolina. He did not rise to his feet and applaud. He was a very slow-moving, slow-speaking man, but deep within him he began to address Father James Anthony Walsh of Boston, as later he was to salute him in letters, "*Carissime.*" He and Father Walsh joined in conversation, which developed into permanent friendship. Father Price became to Father Walsh "Father Fred."

In meeting Father Fred, Father James met a true missioner who impressed on him by his very visible presence how impossible it is to separate the missionary spirit into compartments. It was one, whether it looked to China or North Carolina. And he found himself from that moment confronted with a lifework which differed slightly from what he had first looked on as his task when climbing to his "rookery" in Union Park Street. It was to arouse a general spirit of apostolicity among American Catholics.

The way to do it was to send forth foreign missioners from the United States. Their utter heroism would arouse a corresponding heroism in home missioners. Somebody would have to send them forth, and the sending of them would be in itself a mighty task. Was that task also to be a part of his life's work? It seemed too great.

Some priests in their optimism looked on it as an easy task! Father Elliot of the Paulists, for instance. He pictured to himself a whole happy chapter of future events. Archbishop Farley, of New York, so he had heard, was thinking of establishing a foreign-mission seminary at Troy, New York. The young men of the United States, in whom he had unbounded confidence, would throng to it. Then they would go to Asia or Africa, and would astonish the Europeans (who had too little confidence in American Catholics) by both their enterprise and their patience. Then would American Catholics awake. The wakening would be felt not only outside the United States, but in Wyoming, North Carolina, and the Dakotas.

Father Elliot wanted Father James to put himself behind this seminary: "I am sure you will pardon any air of officiousness in my suggestions. I know that you, who have placed an American diocese foremost in contributing the sinews of God's Holy War, are the one."

Father James looked on the establishment of the seminary as difficult. He was aware of Archbishop Farley's scheme, but knew that it had been dependent on an expectation—somewhat dismal for France—that the Paris Seminary on the *Rue du Bac* might be closed by the anticlerical government, and that some of its staff could emigrate to New York. It was not closed. The government did not wish to export its anticlericalism, and it let some French missioners still be trained in Paris, in the hopes that, even though Christian, they would in foreign parts as Frenchmen heighten French prestige. So it was impossible for Archbishop Farley to staff his proposed seminary. And, besides that, even a seminary could not bring American foreign missions into existence. In addition to missioners, there had to be a mission society to send out missioners. Individually they would be lost.

Father Walsh might, it is true, start a seminary himself, and also a society like Cardinal Vaughan's English one at Mill Hill. But had he the position—he was no prelate—and had he the qualifications? No previous experience seemed to have prepared him for such an enterprise. And then there was the question of time. Time was precious, and he was using the precious time that God gave him for something already assigned to him. To try to do two things at the same time would be to do both of them badly, and would waste time. He preferred therefore to continue to give the time allotted to him to his work at the S. P. F. He would merely try to do his work at 62 Union Park Street in a manner that would encourage interest in all missions at home and abroad. That would mean not doing two things, but doing his one work more intelligently and more fruitfully.

Father Fred Price did not fade from his mind. He was the type of home missioner who could be a model to foreign missioners. He lived among people as ignorant of the Catholic Church as the Chinese, and who, through misinformation, were even more bitterly hostile to it. He was able—through being one of them—to live as a part of the people with whom and for whom he worked. Father Walsh heard stories of how Father Price lived, traveling hundreds of miles on sandy country roads, helping other travelers when their vehicles lost a wheel. He could hobnob with farmers, giving them farmer's advice. He was making himself loved by people whom he loved and who respected him as the true neighbor in spite of their weight of three hundred years of prejudice against his creed. He had built up a mission center at Nazareth, North Carolina, and was radiating a Catholic influence. Wonderful man, even from this center, so far from other Catholic populations, he was editing a magazine, *Truth,* which had attained, far and wide, a circulation of seventeen thousand, and was missionizing the more fortunate Catholics of New York and Boston, Cincinnati and San Francisco.

In the fall of 1905, Father Walsh heard that Father Price's mission in Nazareth, North Carolina, had burned down, and he wrote an article for Father O'Brien's *Sacred Heart Review:*

"A heavy cross has been laid on a truly apostolic priest—one of our own—who has been struggling these many years to bring the true message of Jesus Christ to the people, non-Catholic and Catholic, of North Carolina.

"Father Price, editor of *Truth,* and an ardent and self-sacrificing missionary, has lost, by fire, the accumulation of a lifetime: books, documents, furniture, the whole outfit of his magazine work, including his mailing list.

"The Director had the privilege of meeting this noble soul at the last missionary conference in Washington, and has ever since desired to interest the S. P. F. in his work, the more so because, on that occasion, Father Price expressed publicly his desire to gather some mites in his own impoverished field for the benefit of the world-wide movement.

"Father Price needs books and he needs money. He needs both *badly* and *at once;* and the Propagation of the Faith Office will be only too glad to receive and transmit whatever the heart of a reader may prompt him to give. Already the Diocesan Office has sent $15 to this worthy missioner." [12]

His interest in home missions drew him into correspondence with another priest, Father Francis Clement Kelley, of Lapeer, Michigan—who was later to become Bishop of Oklahoma City and Tulsa, and who is otherwise widely known and widely thanked as founder of the Catholic Church Extension Society. Father Kelley, as did Father Walsh, believed that it was a mistake to separate in one's thoughts the double apostolic task of missions in Dakota and missions in Tonkin, of missions to the Sioux and missions to the Singhalese. He believed that it was even financially a mistake.

Father Kelley—he is still alive and a bishop, and I hope I seem to speak respectfully, as I do—could have, if he had wished, been an inventor. A Prince Edward Islander by birth and Irish by name, he had a Yankee ingenuity with more than a Yankee sense of the invisible. He had a sense of method and a respect for good methods. Merely from the point of view of efficiency, he considered the device for raising money in the United States for missions, as it then worked, as antiquated and wasteful; he was struck by the un-American inefficiency of the system then in vogue. To him it seemed best to have a single money-collecting agency which could collect millions in a lump sum for all missions at home and abroad. He was sure Americans would, American-like, give to it. Then a fourth of the sum could be handed over to the S. P. F., which he was certain would receive five times as much as heretofore. The other three fourths could be used for out-of-the-way parishes in the United States, and for missions to the Indians and to the Negroes.

Father Walsh liked this scheme, and Father Kelley came east to confer with him about it. But the bishops wished to be cautious and postponed acting on it. There were European institutions and European sensibilities to be thought of. So Father Walsh, always discreet with a sense of actuality and humble with a consciousness that he was but one of many, decided to go on for the time being as he had gone on before, trying to raise every year a little larger sum for the S. P. F. in Boston, trying to double thirty thousand into sixty thousand. Such seemed to be all that God permitted.

The Journalist

THERE ARE thoughts which pursue us even though we refuse to act on their prompting. Father Walsh, as he continued at his desk in Union Park Street, could not rid his mind of the thought of an American foreign-mission seminary. He could no more erase it from his consciousness than one could with one's hand smooth the ripple on an eddying stream. The ripple would return. The thought of the foreign-mission seminary was always with him.

When he was collecting money for Father Price's burned-down Nazareth, it was with him; and when he was corresponding with Father Francis C. Kelley of Lapeer, Michigan, concerning more efficient methods of supporting missions in general, it was molesting him.

In the summer of 1906, he went to Europe once again, this time with Father Tracy. It was not for the rest that he crossed the ocean, nor was it this time—as it had been on his second trip—to learn concerning mission activities of Europeans. He had a specific errand. Indeed, he had been sent by Archbishop Williams of Boston, and encouraged by Cardinal Gibbons and Archbishop O'Connell, to arrange with authorities of the

S. P. F. at Paris concerning more advisable allocations of funds to the mission fields in the United States. But his thought of a possible American mission seminary led him to make, while in France, a pilgrimage to the homes of missioners from the Paris Society for Foreign Missions who had died heroic deaths in the pagan lands of the East. It was like visiting the homes of Americans who in some future day might have the same exalted lot. He wanted to be intimate with them. Truly they were in heaven now. Once they had been Frenchmen, but they were not so different from the American missioners whom he hoped to see exist some day. They had become heroes, yet they had had homely, humble, human roots. They had been born somewhere of parents like his own parents. He would visit the ground where they had begun to grow.

Sleeping at the Paris Seminary in the *Rue du Bac,* he found himself occupying a room which had belonged to Henri Dorie. Henri Dorie was a missioner who had been executed in Korea. "Dorie came from the Vendée, from the parish of *Saint Hilaire de Talmont,*" explained Father Delpech. Father Walsh visited the parish.

He visited the home of Gaspard Béchet, whose address he had jotted down in the seminary twenty years before, but which he could still find: 17, *Rue des Machabées, Lyon.*

He visited the early surroundings of Just de Bretenières, near Dijon. He visited those of Peter Chanel, a Marist martyr of Oceania, near the marvelous church at Bourg; and he visited Théophane Vénard's brother, Eusebius, Curé of Assais in Poitiers.

Everywhere he went, there stayed in his thoughts the thought: "If we only had a seminary in America to send out such men, to gladden and save those in darkness!"

He recrossed the Atlantic, and the thought crossed with him. Boston again. It lodged in his brain at Boston.

On October 4, 1906, the Feast of Saint Francis of Assisi, he met with three conspirators who shared the same thought: Father John I. Lane, who had been with him at the seminary at Brighton and had preceded him at Saint Patrick's, and who now, crippled by rheumatism, was praying and suffering as chaplain of the Daly Industrial School in Dorchester; Father Stanton, also a sufferer, an Apollo and a priest; and Father Bruneau, an optimistic French Sulpician, now teaching at the Brighton Seminary. They met at the Daly Industrial School. To themselves they acknowledged their single thought: a foreign-mission seminary!

They confessed it to Archbishop Williams, who was now well over eighty. "It will come," he murmured.

They did not announce it to the public. They merely banded themselves into a vague organization, "The Catholic Foreign Mission Bureau." Directly they would not conspire to establish a seminary. But indirectly they would labor that it be established. They would pray for its coming, and they would stimulate public opinion to demanding it by nourishing the public on various publications.

Concerning the publications, they could be definite. There were to be books, pictures, and a periodical. Father Walsh already had two books ready for the press: *Thoughts from Modern Martyrs,* a collection of excerpts from letters of his

French heroes; and *A Modern Martyr,* his version of Lady Herbert's Life of Théophane Vénard. He was ready to print also *An American Missionary in Alaska,* which was "a most interesting account of the work of Reverend William H. Judge, S. J., by a priest of Saint Sulpice." The periodical should be a bimonthly, and it was to have the romantic—consciously romantic—title of *The Field Afar.* Otherwise they were working in the dark.

This was in October. Before the snow was on the ground, a lady who was a teaching-fellow at Smith College, Massachusetts, Mary Josephine Rogers, a Catholic from Boston, wrote to Father Walsh, whom she did not know, inviting him to come to Smith and speak on Catholic foreign missions. Among the students there was much interest in Protestant missions, and there were a few Catholic students at the college. Even the Protestants wanted to hear of Catholic missions. Soon after writing, Miss Rogers called at Union Park Street. This was a major day in the life of Miss Rogers. Years later she described it:

"It was long years ago that I went to Father Walsh, then Director in Boston of the Society for the Propagation of the Faith, seeking information on foreign missions. I was unknown to him, but in my soul there was already lighted a spark of apostolic fire that awaited the gentle breath of heaven to fan it into a living flame. He was to be that breath.

"I found him at his headquarters on Union Park Street, opposite the Cathedral. Such a surprising, ready-to-tumbledown place it was! Narrow, rickety stairs and a dark hall led to the 'rookery,' as he called his office, and it was with a sense of relief that I saw in the sun's revealing light a room lined with books, here and there on the wall bright splotches of color, a large desk, on the table beside it a globe, and at the desk, smiling a welcome, the Director himself.

"Both room and welcome were characteristic. The room was a garret, sweltering in summer, frigid in winter. It was, however, the office of the Society he represented, and he covered its nakedness and poverty with what he had at hand. Mission souvenirs, curios, pictures, and maps attracted the eye, and Father's compelling personality, his cordial reception, his delightful humor, his frank, normal presentation of the mission cause, captivated the heart. He did not then, nor have I ever known him to do so, appeal simply to the emotions. For emotions are fleeting, and seldom, if ever, lead to divinity of purpose. His was a sensitive nature: he was filled with pity for abandoned babies, ill-treated women, leprous bodies, and all the physical suffering that abounds in our own and pagan lands. He would and did do all in his power to relieve them. But it was the souls of these tortured creatures that called to him, and for them he made appeal.

"I, who had gone in to him as a stranger that day, left him, as hundreds of others have left him, with a warming sense of kinship and a quickened consciousness of a joyful obligation to others, the fulfillment of which would have real value for me only if motivated by a love of souls in Christ."

This was also a major day in the life of Father Walsh, and a major day in the formation of the seminary which aged Archbishop Williams said would come. But at the time he could not see this. He was in the dark. It was but a visit from an intelligent young lady.

On January 1 of the new year, 1907, the first number of *The Field Afar* appeared, its proof having been prepared by Father Lane on his rheumatic bed at the Daly School. It did not belong to the S. P. F., which already had its organ, *The Annals,* translated from a French original. It did not belong to the archdiocese, though it had the enthusiastic approval both of the aged Archbishop Williams and of his coadjutor with right of succession, Archbishop O'Connell. It was a private affair. It aimed at catching the eye of the general reader by its general liveliness, its picturesque pictures and readable stories.

Its first number had some of the characteristics of a first number. It was not printed on as thick and as shiny paper as *The Annals,* which Father Freri, now moved to New York from Baltimore, was editing with new energy. Its front picture, "Catholic Missionaries in Japan," was a little bit blurred. Under the magazine's title was printed the statement: "Devoted to the Interest of Catholic Missions." As its crest was set the very antique, venerable symbol *Chi Rho,* which had appeared in the catacombs, standing for the two first letters in Greek of the name of Christ. Around the *Chi Rho* was inscribed a circle, which of old had stood for eternity but which had come to refer also to the wholeness and sphericity of this earth. Its motto, printed in both English and Latin, was taken from Romans viii, 28: "To those who love God, all things work together for good." Its table of contents did not disclose any apparent novelty: "Editorials; Rev. James Feeney,

C. SS. R.; The Church's Need in Japan; Night at the *Missions Étrangères;* Early New England;" and so forth. It seemed like just another missionary publication.

Perhaps it was possible to discern an experienced canniness in the choice of materials. The Reverend James Feeney had once been a priest at the Redemptorist church, known as the Mission Church, in Roxbury. He had gone to Puerto Rico three years before, and now he was dead. He was Boston news. And so was it Boston news to tell of the work of Father Rasle among the Abenakis of the eighteenth century, under the caption "Early New England." The periodical emanated from Boston. Charity begins at home, but does not end there. Boston news was being tied to the news of the whole planet.

But really *The Field Afar* was an innovation. It was new not so much by its choice of news, as by its tone of telling the news. It adopted an American accent. It suited American tastes.

Americans, reading too rapidly, liked photographs. They liked to see. *The Field Afar* would show them pictures, which could instruct the cursory reader. During his recent trip to France, Father Walsh had used his camera. He had taken a snapshot of the "Castle at Bretenières which belonged to the family from which Just de Bretenières had gone to Tonkin." It was reproduced in *The Field Afar*—what fine homes the French martyrs were ready to leave! At Paris he had encountered a young missioner, Father Lamonnerie, just starting for China. He had invited him to send pictures of China to Boston for the Bostonians.

This was a somewhat new request to a missioner. Not having a camera, he had to delay. He wrote a letter which was published in the first number of *The Field Afar:* "At Paris you asked me to send you some interesting photographs when I should be on my mission. I am anxious to do my best to fulfill this promise. If you still desire such material, and if you are in a position to send the apparatus, I will with much pleasure employ the few moments I have on my mission and on my journeys to take some photographs."

Americans also like humor. They like speeches to begin with a laughable story. Maybe they are wrong, but that is the way they are. And Father Walsh treated Americans the way they were.

This came out particularly in Father Walsh's own contributions to *The Field Afar,* which were accounts of searchings in France for the roots of the lives of French martyrs. He reverenced the martyrs. He liked the French. But there was a place for laughter in these accounts, because, for all his affection for the French and his growing familiarity with them, he was aware that there was a laughable gap between French and American ways. He himself made the laughable mistakes of a traveler, and could laugh at himself. And the French made their mistakes about him. It was hard for the pious housekeepers of French village priests ever to think of him, a priest without a cassock, as wholly orthodox. So he could laugh at them. His laughter was not derisive: it was humble and friendly, even affectionate. Although he was bent on a pious errand, even to nothing less august than the blood of martyrs, he was pursuing that errand through circumstances quaint, homely, and picturesque, and was encountering trivial

THE FIRST DEPARTURE OF MARYKNOLL MISSIONERS, SEPTEMBER 7, 1918

adventures which made one smile at life's little ironies. And why not smile?

He brought these ironies and smiles into his book. They were a part of it as they were a part of life. They were particularly a part of his literary style, which was playful and familiar, and not given to oratorical solemnity. He hinted his reverences in a way that took one off one's guard.

He smiled with his readers. Americans like to smile at French railroad trains, and at French railroad stations, and at the *chef de gare* with his whistle. And he smiled:

" '*En voiture, Messieurs, en voiture, s'il vous plait.*' It was the signal to start, and the mighty ruler of the train was unusually gracious considering the fact that he had no first-class passengers to conduct. I sighed gratefully, reflecting that the heated air would soon be fanned. We waited ten minutes longer, however, before the picayune whistle blew, and the caravan for Bourg was on its way." [13]

Walking in Lyons was not exactly like walking in Boston. There was more curiosity from windows. He was trying to find Gaspard Béchet's mother at *17, Rue des Machabées.*

"I had my way, and we found the street, *Rue des Machabées,* after a short walk. We passed along quickly until we came to Number 17. It was a new apartment house, and the rough brick, fresh from the kiln, had not yet been covered with cement, although several families were evidently installed. There was no answer to our knock, but after some skirmishing in dark courts, which, had I been alone, would have made me feel like a book agent or a thief, we managed to draw a head from one of the lower windows. 'Does Madame Béchet live here?' we asked.

"And the reply came quickly, accompanied by a suspicious look: 'There is no one of that name in this neighborhood.' By this time other windows were occupied with interested auditors, from whose eyes the final vestiges of sleep were just disappearing, and an impromptu council of the court was held. No one had ever heard of the lady. And no one had ever heard of her son, the martyr."

Then he finally did find Madame Béchet, and she was touched by having an American ask after her son.

"The poor mother's eyes filled with tears. She could not speak at first, but, rising, called my attention to several photographs of Gaspard which hung on the walls of the little room. One taken before his departure from the Paris Seminary, another in the group which the Curé had just given me, and a third in Oriental dress. 'Oh, it was hard to lose him,' she said at length; 'so hard to be old and alone without him!' He was her only child, she told me. . . ."

He visited the homes of half-a-dozen other martyrs, among them the one whose personality had most charmed him in his student days, Théophane Vénard. He found Eusebius, the Curé of Assais, Théophane's brother.

"In the Curé's garden at Assais there was a little family of turtledoves. I learned of their existence at four o'clock on the morning after my arrival. Their cooing was low and sweet, but not soothing enough to let me forget the world again, so I lay awake, and, recalling the events of the preceding day, tried to realize my surroundings as the guest of a martyr's brother. Towards six o'clock I heard the firm step of Father

Eusebius as he came slowly up the winding stairs and with rapid movement approached the door of my chamber, which received a knock more vigorous than was necessary. A few minutes later the *Angelus* rang, and in another quarter of an hour I found my way into the church, saluting, as I passed, my early serenaders in their cage."

The Field Afar very soon began to receive verbal compliments. Archbishop O'Connell remarked: "It is certainly gratifying to testify to its great improvement upon the sort of missionary literature we were accustomed to not so very long ago." [14]

All the way from University College, Dublin, Ireland, the classical scholar, Father Henry Brown, S. J., wrote to Father Walsh: "You have evidenced a completely new spirit, and your work is an object lesson for the whole English-speaking world. God knows it was badly wanting."

Then there were other kinds of compliments. Before two years were out, his periodical had five thousand subscribers. One of them was John Fong Ying, of Boston's Chinatown. All that they each had to pay was fifty cents, but a compliment which is made at the cost of money has a healthy monetary ring to it.

Two hundred and seventy-five foreign missioners began to send letters. That was a compliment, and it provided news.

Finally a number of young ladies complimented the periodical by volunteering to work for it. Most conspicuous among them was the same Miss Mary Rogers of Smith College who had visited Father Walsh's office in the fall of 1906. In the winter of 1907, she had brought him successfully to lecture at Smith, and in the following summer had returned to live with her family near Boston at Jamaica Plain. She was busy teaching during the hours of day, except in summer, but out of hours she became busier, preparing photographs in order that they could be reproduced. And there were so many letters to read. There was so much correspondence. *The Field Afar* had an office of its own now in Malden Street, near the Cathedral. It was a convenient compliment to have ladies volunteering to help, particularly the most constant one, Miss Mary Rogers.

Things were going so well that a whisper came to the heart of Father Walsh: "Since there is so much growing interest in the missions, why not start the desired seminary to meet the interest?" Miss Mary Donovan, a secretary in his office, wanted to become a missionary, but there was no way for an American girl to enter the missions. She had to go to Canada, learn French, join a French order, the Immaculate Conception Sisters, in order to be sent to China, there to work in a hospital.

The Archdiocese of Boston was so much more conscious of foreign missions now that it was giving seventy thousand dollars a year to the S. P. F.

The whole country was becoming more conscious of the whole world. Since the War with Spain and the march of the American Marines to Peking in the Boxer Rebellion, and President Roosevelt's peace-making between Russia and Japan, the United States was being recognized as a world power. The United States had new prestige in the East, but it had no Catholic prestige and was counted in the Orient as utterly Protestant. This piqued the Catholics. They did not like to hear it said that American missioner was synonymous with Protestant missionary. European Catholics remarked with helpful frankness that American Catholics were too soft to be missioners.

Father Walsh made the most of this disparagement of the hardihood of American Catholics. He appealed to American Catholics' self-respect, writing in 1909 in *The Sacred Heart Review*.

"Are our boys less worthy, less courageous, and less heroic in sacrificing the amenities and conveniences of civilized life, to leave father and mother, and a dear home, to follow Christ and His Apostles, and the many thousands of staunch confessors and martyrs? Our faith is just as precious as that of the first Christians; it is the same in source, in strength, in divinity." [15]

Not only American women like Mary Donovan were stirring themselves to enter the mission field, but young men. A general missionary society of religious priests and Brothers with headquarters in Holland, the Society of the Divine Word, was establishing a recruiting house in Techny, Illinois, to receive the recruits.

The Pope himself, the saintly Pius X, had given the signal to American Catholics to play a world part by declaring, on June 29, 1908, that the United States had ceased canonically to be a country ranked as a mission. It could now be missioner-sending.

Archbishop O'Connell of Boston had spoken the sentiment of the American hierarchy at a Mission Congress in 1909 at Chicago:

"The providential hour of opportunity has struck. We must be up and doing. All indications point to our great vocation as a missionary nation. To be recreant to such a high calling is to abdicate a blessed vantage ground and to undo gradually the good work which has already been accomplished in this land by the apostolic zeal of the Church's followers. Our country has already reached out beyond her boundaries and is striving to do a work of extension of American civic ideals for other peoples. Shall it be said that the Church in this land has been outstripped by the civil power under which we live?" [16]

Voices from outside were continuing to suggest to Father Walsh that he found a seminary. One of the voices was that of a Dominican exiled from France, Father Cothonay. He urged the editor of *The Field Afar* to begin with a corps of instructors made up of other exiled French Dominicans. Another voice, Bishop Benziger of Quilon, India, suggested something similar.

But Father Walsh still felt unfitted for the task. He did not have complete confidence in himself or a confidence that God intended him for the work. Let the Carmelites keep on praying that God's will be done. He had a cousin, Sister Eleanor, among the Carmelites in Roxbury. Mother Beatrix, the Superior in Roxbury, one of the unknown founders of the permanence of our country, was ever praying for American missioners. His brother, Timothy, had been the architect of the Roxbury Convent of Carmel on Mt. Pleasant Avenue. He would rather trust much to Carmel, and little to his puny journalism.

In the summer of 1910, he again visited Europe, partly for more reporting, mostly for medical treatment.

Then in September, 1910, came the International Eucharistic Congress at Montreal, Canada, the first of such congresses to be held in the New World. He was back in time to be one of those who could rejoice in it by being present at it.

Another priest who was present at the Congress was Father Price of North Carolina. Discovering by chance that the editor of *The Field Afar,* whom he had never forgotten, was also there, he telephoned him in great haste, and caught him on the telephone only a few minutes before the great outdoor Mass was to be celebrated on Fletcher's Field.

"How is it?" asked Father Walsh over the telephone. "You wish to see me now? But I am starting for Fletcher's Field."

"But I must see you first. I will be with you in an instant." A Southerner made haste. He had cause.

And he was with Father Walsh in an instant. And their conversation began. It was not interrupted by the Mass, although it became silent during it. It continued during the Mass—transfigured, without words. After the Mass it continued in the lobby of the Windsor Hotel, and there fell back into words. They talked as if they were alone in the desert, oblivious of the hotel and its leather chairs, and its gilding, and the messenger boys: "Paging Father Flanagan! Paging Father Milbank! Paging Abbé Rigaud!" Once a prelate who knew both of them well, Bishop Donahue of Wheeling, West Virginia, came smiling up to them. He might have been as far away as the smiling moon, and as unremarked.

Together they gained a courage which neither of them had separately. Together they assumed a boldness of plan which neither of them dared to have alone. They would start a seminary themselves!

"At this first Eucharistic Congress in the New World . . ." They shook hands. "We will found a seminary."

"*Walsh and Price*"

AT THIS TIME those who were friendly enough with Fathers Walsh and Price to be able to indulge in banter began to refer to them as "Walsh & Price." They were like partners in a promoting concern: "Walsh & Price."

They were indeed partners in a common project, and were —as I am told partners should be—not duplicates. Father Price was six years older, taller of height, larger of frame, broader of shoulder, slower of speech, slower of stride. And their derivations were different. I do not refer to any definite differences in blood, for such differences are not definite. Father Walsh can be called of Irish race, but one grandmother had been an Englishwoman, Elizabeth Holmes, who had visited Ireland and become a convert to the Catholic Faith. Father Price can be called English, but as many bloods mingle in English blood as languages in the English language. But their traditions were definitely different, and so were their upbringings.

Father Price was a Southerner, Father Walsh a Northerner. They looked at the City of Washington with their heads turned from different directions. One was a city lad, the other a country boy. Father Price came of a family of Catholic converts in a State, North Carolina, where there were almost no Catholics. Father Walsh came from a family of Irish immigrants, Catholics, who could not imagine being other than Catholic and who lived gregariously with other Catholics in overcrowded parishes.

Yet Divine Providence had led them into similar paths.

Father Price had definitely clinched his decision to be a priest when, during a shipwreck from which there seemed to be no chance of rescue, he had offered his life to Our Lady should he be saved. Father Walsh had decided definitely to be a priest when he was treading the very solid ground of the Harvard Yard.

They differed in disposition and aptitudes. Father Walsh, had he not become a priest, might have become a witty journalist, quick to take into account the mood of the public. Father Price, had he not been a priest, might have been the owner of a plantation, quick to take into account the mood of the seasons. As a priest Father Price had a leaning toward a contemplative vocation. Father Walsh was for action.

Yet God's ordering had led them into similar paths. Both had become zealous apostles. Both had dedicated their main attention to missions. Both, in the furthering of missions, had taken up journalism. Both had had great experience in the collecting of alms. Both had traveled, though Father Price had traveled only in the United States. Both had been given a great reliance on prayer: one could pray like a Carmelite; the other could pray with Carmelites.

And now they both were ready to burn their bridges behind

them and go on to the adventure of establishing what they considered to be their country's greatest need, a Catholic foreign-mission seminary. For the time being Father Walsh had to continue at Boston with the S. P. F., but it was only for the time being. Father Price handed over his mission house in Nazareth to others.

Their first task was of a diplomatic nature. It was to gain ecclesiastical approval of their undertaking: first from the American hierarchy, and then from the Holy See at Rome. They well knew that as mere individuals they could do nothing. The Church was a family bound together in its myriad parts. Their private conviction that they were bent on something supremely good was a mere private conviction.

Father Price, being the one of the partnership the more free, had to take the lead. He began by a visit to Archbishop O'Connell of Boston, who had succeeded Archbishop Williams on the latter's death in 1907. To Archbishop O'Connell he was far from being a stranger, for they had been students together at Saint Charles's Seminary in Maryland, and the Archbishop still remembered Father Price as an unforgettable companion, unequaled for charm and spirituality, with whom to take a walk had been real recreation. The Archbishop greeted him as an old friend and made of him a new friend. In his memoirs he has left us an account of how happy was their meeting:

"To me it was a privilege to listen as, with gentle voice and ever-present smile, he outlined the wonderful plan he had, by reflection of years, defined in the most sensible, practical, yet supernatural inspiration. He valued, beyond their merits, the few suggestions I offered, and prized, beyond its value, the financial aid I was able to give him. We renewed memories of our delightful comradeship of the long ago, and when he had left me I had the perfectly assured feeling that I had talked with a saint, whom God and His Blessed Mother had preserved for the initiation and carrying out of a great plan, conceived and executed to the glory of God, the spread of the Gospel of Christ, and the love of His holy Mother Mary." [17]

Archbishop O'Connell approved. This was much. Boston's Archbishop had the reputation of making clean-cut decisions. He did not like schemes vague and romantic. What was impossible, he brushed aside. What he considered possible, he took up with rare vigor. He was strong. His approval was definite, yet weighted with sagacious admonitions. He was not in favor of having the seminary at Washington, D. C., for it was too far from the centers of Catholic population. He was in favor of having American priests teach the American boys who volunteered as missioners. He would be glad to have the seminary in his diocese. There would be, he believed, many vocations there.

Next Father Price went to Cardinal Gibbons at Baltimore— at that time the only American Cardinal. Then he visited the Apostolic Delegate at Washington, Archbishop Falconio. Both prelates gave him every encouragement, but pointed out that all would depend on the attitude of the American hierarchy when it met at its annual gathering in Washington, at the Catholic University, in the spring of 1911.

In the meantime Father Price, who wore out rosaries with his North Carolina fingers, said his rosary; and Father Walsh, still working through *The Field Afar,* sent out in it leaflets requesting prayers. And meanwhile, also, Father Price traveled about the country from bishop to bishop, acquainting them with the project they were going to have to consider. And he and Father Walsh prepared a statement of their plan, and forwarded it to Cardinal Gibbons.

Cardinal Gibbons forthwith wrote a letter dated Lady Day, March 25, 1911, which he himself sent to the bishops, in the phraseology of which we can see traces of what Father Walsh had been saying for a decade:

"That such a seminary is needed, and urgently, seems daily more evident. The prestige of our country has become widespread; and Protestants, especially in the Far East, are profiting by it, to the positive hindrance of Catholic missioners. I understand that even the educated classes in China, misled by the almost complete absence of American Catholic priests, believe that the Church of Rome has no standing in America.

"Conscious that we are still short of priests in many dioceses, I would cite the words of Cardinal Manning referring to the foundation of Mill Hill.

"It is quite true that we have need of men and means at home; and it is 'because we have need of men, of more men and more means, by a great deal, than we as yet possess, that I am convinced we ought to send both men and means abroad. . . . If we desire to find the surest way to multiply immensely our own material means for works at home, it is by not limiting the expansion of charity and by not paralyzing the zeal of self-denial.' "

Cardinal Gibbons not only recommended the scheme, but

he recommended the two priests who were to put it in action:

"Father Walsh is a priest of the Boston Archdiocese. He was ordained in 1892, and the late revered Archbishop Williams appointed him, more than eight years ago, Diocesan Director for the Propagation of the Faith. Under His Grace, Archbishop O'Connell, Father Walsh has been confirmed in this position, which he still holds. He also directs the Catholic Foreign Mission Bureau, editing *The Field Afar* and issuing other publications bearing on the subject of foreign missions.

"Father Price has spent twenty-five years in difficult mission work. He is the Superior of the Apostolate of Secular Priests of North Carolina and editor of the magazine, *Truth.*"

On the twenty-seventh of April, the archbishops of the United States were to meet in Washington. Up till the last minute, Father Price was going here and there promoting his project. On April 18 he telegraphed to Father Walsh:

CARISSIME:
I am back in Baltimore with my sleeves rolled up for business. Your friend and servant in Our Lord.

T. F. P.

Then the hierarchy met in Caldwell Hall of the Catholic University. Into the hall Father Price was not bidden, for he was no archbishop, but he stayed outside, taking his part in the deliberations by saying his rosary. Hours passed and the doors remained closed, and he imagined that the project sponsored by "Walsh & Price" was undergoing endless debate.

Then the doors opened. He made inquiries. It turned out that the project had been approved straightway with little discussion, and that the long hours had been spent on other matters. No one had bothered to come out and tell him of the fate of what was so dear to his heart. It had not occurred to anyone that he was walking up and down with such patient impatience. Evidently not every one took the matter as seriously as he, or as Father Walsh of Boston.

He telegraphed to Father Walsh the good news. Then he took the train to Nazareth, North Carolina, where he still had some affairs to settle. Seated at his dear Nazareth, which he had decided to quit for a work which seemed even more vital, he did not on this evening regret the decision he had made. He was filled with hope for the future of the seminary. He was looking to the future, and he penned a letter to Father Walsh, the sharer of his future hopes, even before he lay down to sleep. It began:

Carissime:

"This is the day which the Lord has made. Let us be glad and rejoice in it! As I telegraphed you, the archbishops adopted the indorsement which we had prepared—passed it without friction of any kind and unanimously. The Cardinal tells me that the location is left free in our hands. . . . The Cardinal had previously told me to leave out of the paper anything referring to location, and I had a talk with each of the archbishops before the meeting. I expected to be called in at the meeting, as the Cardinal told me he would send for me to explain matters, but there was no need, as I had previously given the archbishops an 'organizer's plan' and so was not called, and the matter passed before I knew it. . . . I am going to have a lot of Masses and prayers said in thanksgiving. I am very happy!"

Immediately a request was printed by Father Walsh in his *Field Afar:*

"In the meantime we ask our readers to join with us in prayer of thanksgiving for what has already been accomplished, and to continue their remembrance, that the organizers of the new seminary may be guided in the matter of location and in the many details incidental to so important a work.

"Prayer has thus far accomplished so much, that I appeal especially for this form of help." [18]

And now there had to be the journey to Rome. Archbishop O'Connell, seeing that things were really going ahead, released Father Walsh from his work in the Boston Archdiocese as Director of the S. P. F., and gave him a letter to Bishop Thomas F. Kennedy, Rector of the North American College in Rome, in which he also asked the Bishop to give Father Walsh a letter of introduction to Monsignor Laurenti, Secretary of the Congregation of *Propaganda Fide.* He also gave Father Walsh a letter of introduction to the Papal Secretary of State, Cardinal Merry del Val.

Father Walsh turned over his office at the S. P. F. to Father Joseph F. McGlinchey, D. D., another priest of Boston who had become fired with zeal for foreign missions, and who in years to come was to have his brother Henry die as a Jesuit missioner in India. He had translated from the Italian a book by Father Manna called *The Workers are Few,* which, like Father Walsh's writings, had been an invitation for mission vocations. Father Walsh did not give up his *Field Afar.* That belonged still to his Catholic Mission Bureau. He planned to have it become the organ of his future seminary. In its June number he saluted Father McGlinchey as bringing to his work "a strong interest in the mission cause and an intelligent zeal."

In doing anything for the last time, there is a sadness. For eight years now Father Walsh had been Director of the S. P. F., growing used to his "rookery." Now he was flying elsewhere. And mightn't it be a wild-goose chase?

One person did not think it was any such thing. Father André, still at Avignon in France, was still enough a Bostonian to take the Boston *Pilot,* and still enough a friend of the foreign missions and of Father Walsh to take *The Field Afar.* He read in them concerning what Father Walsh was now doing, and on May 22 wrote to him:

"With whole pleasure I saw, in your paper and in the *Pilot,* the announcement of a seminary for foreign missions and your appointment to the direction of it!

"I thank God with all my heart, and I congratulate you. You will have trouble of course, and crosses, but what a splendid work, what a magnificent mission for you! Your zeal so generously spent in the propagation of the Faith is acknowledged and rewarded.

"I cannot tell you, as I would wish, my joy and my hope . . . you will do great things. Our Lord has chosen you as His instrument for the glory of the American Church. . . .

"Goodby, dear Father Walsh. Our Lord bless you and your grand work!"

If Father Walsh received this letter before sailing for

Europe, he must have been embarrassed by it. It was so optimistic. It treated him as if he were already at the head of a seminary. Where was the seminary?

But I doubt if he did receive it before he sailed. It was written at Avignon eight days before his sailing date, May 30, and though there were such things as five-day steamers—the *Lusitania* and *Mauretania*—they did not sail from Avignon or arrive at Boston. Probably, when on May 30 he boarded the Cunarder, the *Franconia,* in East Boston, he had not opened the letter as yet.

Where was Father Price? Had he been delayed at the ferry? He was the other partner of "Walsh & Price," and he was necessary to the party, but he had not arrived. The boat whistled. Father Walsh was not looking out to sea over the harbor islands, or back at Boston's hill. He was scanning the gangplank for a lost sheep. Where was the calm Southerner, slow-moving, patient as a tree, Father Price?

At the last moment Father Price walked slowly up the gangplank—nothing fretful or Yankee about him. He was carrying his own bag, and he could carry it, and he wanted to carry it, for it was light and also valuable because it contained little besides a few papers. He had never crossed the ocean before. He handed over to Father Walsh two United States bank notes and a few checks. Father Walsh could now take charge. Father Walsh was used to European travel, and knew about money affairs and knew French. For six months he, Father Price, had been the more active; it was Father Walsh's turn.

The *Franconia* sailed with "Walsh & Price" aboard; and a week later it was veering round the smooth, green headlands of Ireland. On June 8 it passed the tide-sucked buoys at the entrance of Liverpool Harbor. "Walsh & Price" immediately made their way to the foreign-mission seminary—Saint Peter's Preparatory Seminary at Freshfield, outside of Liverpool, a branch of the deceased Cardinal Vaughan's Mill Hill.

Then on to London, where they lodged at the center of Mill Hill under the hospitality of its robust, bearded Superior, Father Henry.

Then on to Paris, where they stayed but a day and yet had time to visit the seminary in the *Rue du Bac,* and to pray near the relics of Théophane Vénard, who by now had been beatified and was known throughout the world as the Blessed Théophane, and in *The Field Afar* as "our martyr." From Paris Father Walsh wrote a letter home to Boston:

"In Paris—arrived last night. Same old place—hardly stranger to me now than New York—except when it is up to me to do the *parlez* business—and then I have to pinch myself.

"Father Price is getting a new shock about every quarter of an hour although much escapes him—since he is not of this world—(not as much, I fear, as his companion). But some one has to be alive—and I seem destined to be the distracted one.

"My health has been 'not too bad.' The 'tired feeling' hangs on somewhat, and probably will till after the Roman experience is over. We shall be in Rome—at least we expect to be—before this letter arrives. . . .

". . . We know not the future. At present I feel absolutely unworthy, not to say unfit, to go on with this great work—and that I can be no more than a passing agent through whom

FATHER WALSH BELOW DECKS ON A RIVER JUNK IN
SOUTH CHINA

God will work. We are both depending almost entirely on prayer, and I on the prayers of others. As for Father Price, he seems to enjoy his prayers much more than any other exercise or recreation. We hardly have time to compare notes. Just now he is out buying a stock of necessaries—to be thrown away when used. His bag is full of manuscripts, but this is about all he carries with him. . . ."

On the evening of the fifteenth, they took the night train from Paris. In the morning, Switzerland. They descended at Lausanne to celebrate Mass. Then on they shot for ten more hours under the weight of Alpine mountains, by the Simplon tunnel, to Italy. A stop at Milan had to be made because there also was a foreign-mission seminary, and at its head Bishop Vigano. On the morning of June 18, 1911, they started southward for Rome.

It was Father Price's first visit to Italy, but not Father Walsh's. They looked out the windows. This was the plain of Lombardy. They craned their necks to see the names of the railroad stations. *Piacenza, Parma*—the names were familiar. Then came the great railroad junction of Bologna.

In the Middle Ages the pilgrims had walked and ridden to Rome with an awe which beat in their hearts, and so pulsated in their bodies that it set their very voices in cadence:

> *O Roma nobilis, orbis et domina,*
> *Cunctarum urbium excellentissima,*
> *Roseo martyrum sanguine rubea,*
> *Albis et virginum liliis candida,*
> *Salutem dicimus tibi per omnia,*
> *Te benedicimus, salve per saecula.*

It was not so much that Rome was a city great in palaces and churches, encrusted with gold and marble—for in the Middle Ages Constantinople stood for riches—but it was enduring, and it was precious with its stain of martyrs' blood, and splendid with its holy whiteness of the lilies of virgins. And it was majestic and ruling because the memories and relics of Saints Peter and Paul were there:

> *Petre, tu prepotens coelorum claviger,*
> *Vota, precantium exaudi iugiter.*
>
> *　　　*　　　*　　　*
>
> *O Paule, suscipe nostra precamina,*
> *Cuius philosophos vicit industria.*

And there in Rome on Saint Peter's throne, on the Fisherman's seat, sat the successors of Saint Peter, with the most tremendous, heartbreakingly tender authority that human beings ever could possess.

No wonder that in the Middle Ages the very thought of traveling evoked the thought of Rome as the goal of all travel. "All roads lead to Rome." A roamer was one who went Romewards. Whither else was it worth-while traveling with all the hardships of travel? Whither else except to the Holy Land, which made one a palmer?

"Walsh & Price" were now roamers to Rome.

> *O Roma nobilis, orbis et domina!*

Now the wheels of the railroad train were beating out the cadence of the old tenth-century marching hymn.

The successor to Saint Peter at Rome was now Pope Pius X. A majority of the successors of Saint Peter had suffered violent deaths in this turbulent, rebellious, and often penitential world. There was little likelihood that Pope Pius would join the list of martyrs. But it was already recognized that he was one of the holy Popes. He had an utter simplicity which united him to other holy Popes across the ages. Diplomats might say that he did not understand diplomacy. He acknowledged that he did not, and was therefore the diplomat par excellence. Heretics and some proud Catholics might say that he was ignorant. He was as ignorant as Saint Peter, and as wise. He was of as humble birth as Saint Peter, a postman's son. He was the eternal Pope, supremely a Servant of the Servants of God.

O Roma nobilis, orbis et domina!

The train was darting through tunnel after tunnel in the Apennines. It was hot June, but the car window was best left shut against the smoke that would pour in if it were open during the tunnel transit.

Truly they were going as pilgrims to Rome, to the Father of Christendom, but they were seeking more than to pray; they were seeking justice. And it was not so much to the Holy Father that they were appealing as to the Sacred Congregation of Propaganda. There was a saying that always one could secure justice from the Congregations of Rome if one persevered, but one had to be sure that one's cause was just. Was not their cause just?

Was it not for the good of the Holy See that it accept and approve this offer from the New World? So it seemed.

The great trial of the pontificate of this holy, simple Pope had been his quarrel with the eldest daughter of the Church, France—or rather, with the atheistic ruling clique of that

nation. It was distressing that the government of France had
made the Church in France poor, but it was far more distressing to receive the insults from the representatives of a nation
which in his heart the Pope especially loved. France in the
nineteenth century had been mysteriously the great missionary
nation. It seemed that now, with her vocations cut off and
many of her religious exiled, she would be crippled in her
missionary work. Why should not, then, the Pope welcome
"Walsh & Price" with their American project as God-sent?
They were presenting him with the prospect of a missionary
United States.

But who knows?

How much did the Pope himself, in spite of his holiness,
know of the United States? And how much did the prelates
of the various Congregations to whom he delegated authority?

Father Walsh had traveled enough in Europe to know that
many Europeans did not know what language was spoken by
the citizens of the United States. Was it Spanish? Or English?
They often asked about buffaloes and about Red Indians. No
Pope had ever visited the United States. No Pope had ever
visited the Western Hemisphere except Pope Pius X, who,
before becoming Pope, had set foot in South America. Would
they—"Walsh & Price"—receive justice in Rome? And how
did they know their cause was just?

It was toward dusk that they arrived in the Eternal City,
and they stepped from the train as ghosts, dim and unreal in
the dim twilight. It was Rome that seemed real, Rome and the
past, and not they. In their dimness they had no appearance
of being dignitaries. They were not dignitaries. Seen in an

open space or by a street-lamp, they showed as very ordinary men and, though priests with the priestly collar, yet in sub-priestly attire, jacketed like American businessmen, with wintry but not sacerdotal hats, and no cassocks. They had some Latin in their minds, but only enough Italian to elicit questions from a cab driver. It was a Sunday night. So late it was that they hesitated to knock at the door of any early-to-bed, wise, ecclesiastic. They lodged at the Hotel Minerva, a hostelry of which they had heard as possessing clerical traditions, where there was even a chapel. Then on Monday morning they sought the hospitality of the North American College. Bishop Kennedy received them cordially, but he had no room for them. He sent them to the Sulpician Seminary. No room. He sent them to the Rector of the English Church of San Silvestro, who took them in and gave them a roof.

Then they brushed up, tried to look clerical and orthodox, even without cassocks, and descended the sloping sidewalks with sinking hearts to the *Piazza di Spagna*. There stood the column that commemorates the promulgation of the dogma of Our Lady's Immaculate Conception, and there the flower venders were trying to keep their flowers from being burned up by the June sun by protecting them with parasols, and there stood the dignified seventeenth-century building of Propaganda, under the jurisdiction of which fell all the Church's missionary enterprises. They entered the building and asked for Monsignor Laurenti, Secretary of Propaganda.

The Monsignor received them with Roman graciousness, and made them feel at home by talking to them in English. Secretly he was rather impressed with the twain, but secretly also he could not help wondering if mercurial, hustling North Americans could ever have the stamina and patience for the slow, unrewarded life of foreign missioners. He could arrange for an interview for them with Cardinal Gotti, the head of Propaganda, but not now. They would better, before the interview, get in touch with the Reverend Doctor Schut, of the Mill Hill Society, who was resident at Rome. He could coach them and interpret for them: Cardinal Gotti spoke no English.

Cardinal Gotti in turn received these strange unplumaged beings from North America, them and Doctor Schut. He kept his private thoughts urbanely hid after the manner of wise prelates, and yet surveyed them through and through, possibly noticing that Father Price was paying less attention to him than to his own rosary (an elbow showed his fingers were moving). Father Price did no talking. Cardinal Gotti invited the two to come again with a written plan which he could submit to the Congregation of Propaganda, and this they did. After that there interposed a wait, an ecclesiastical wait.

During the wait Father Price went to the Holy House at Loretto, there to pray to Our Lady. Father Walsh visited various important prelates: Cardinal Merry del Val, and Monsignor Bonzano, the latter Rector of Urban College, belonging to Propaganda, at which native priests from heathen lands were being trained, and native priests had for centuries been trained. Father Walsh was seeking advice. There was much advice needed.

On June 29, the Feast of Saints Peter and Paul, the two were summoned for a third visit to Cardinal Gotti. This time he was happy to tell them that Propaganda approved their plan.

This was the decisive day on which bells rang in their hearts. It was the real birthday of their enterprise.

Then came another day, no less necessary, and outwardly more impressive. On June 30 they were presented to the Holy Father, Pius X. Here is Father Walsh's account of what happened:

"Pius X was at his desk making a few notes; but, before we could finish our triple genuflections, he extended his hand for obeisance, and indicated our seats for the interview.

"We had prepared a brief outline of our purpose in coming to Rome. Pius X adjusted his glasses and began to read it. As he continued, his face seemed to grow very serious. Evidently His Holiness had not been prepared for our visit, and was surprised at the idea of *Americans* going out to convert pagans in mission lands. At once, however, he remarked that work for pagans abroad would react favorably on the work of the Church in America, and he continued his close reading of the outline.

"Suddenly the fine face of the saintly Pontiff lighted with a smile. He laid our papers on his desk and, turning squarely toward us, joined his hands as with evident pleasure, and said, *'Ma é finito!*—Why, it is all settled!' We were at the end of our quest, not at the beginning as His Holiness had thought; and our audience then meant only a pleasant interchange of greetings with good wishes and a paternal counsel from the Father of Christendom.

"As we arose from our knees after the blessing and backed towards the door, Pius X, smiling, accompanied his *Addio* with a repeated relaxed movement of both hands, and made us feel the children that we were in the presence of our kindly spiritual Father.

"Our cup of joy was full as we crossed the square and entered again the great Basilica of the Apostle." [19]

There they knelt and prayed beside the rail that encloses the great altar and the tombs of Saints Peter and Paul beneath it. They prayed with the most typical part of Christian prayer —thanksgiving. Time faded into nothing, and they were back in the days of the first Apostles, they who were following in those Apostles' footsteps, carrying on the great task.

O Roma nobilis, orbis et domina!

After that they left Rome, and for a moment they parted.

Father Walsh went to a mission house of Mill Hill in the Tyrol, at Brixen, where he could study mission seminaries, and where he also could rest. Then he went to France as if to visit his friend, Théophane Vénard, to tell him of what had happened and ask his help. It was not Théophane that he could see in the flesh, but he could see his surroundings, which were like a part of him left here on earth, like a cloak which he had once worn. He saw Théophane's brother once again. The days of Father Eusebius were drawing to a close. The light of his life's day was fading. "I will never see you again on this earth," said the brother. The day of Father Walsh's task on earth was, however, dawning. He was going on with Théophane's task, which Théophane's brother had helped him to understand.

Father Price took a different path. He went to Lourdes in France, there at the Grotto of Our Lady's apparition, where she had said, "I am The Immaculate Conception," to find his rest and refreshment and even instruction. He, too, had reverence for Blessed Théophane Vénard, but it was the little girl who had seen the apparition who was more in his thoughts, Bernadette Soubirous. She had grown up and been a nun at Nevers, and had there been buried. She was not yet canonized, but it was as if, in going to see her, he could see what she had seen, and he went to Nevers, where lay her body. From then on he had such devotion for Bernadette that he began to be called "Father Bernadette." Some very deep experience at Lourdes had come to him. He never explained exactly what it was but intimated: "Things could never be the same to me again."

Then the two came together at Liverpool, and sailed for Boston—"Walsh & Price"!

Hawthorne

Fathers Walsh and Price were no longer "Walsh & Price, promoters." They were now an accredited Society of two with ecclesiastical warrant, known as the Catholic Foreign Mission Society of America.

The name was a grand one, and they had chosen it carefully, in order that there might be no mistaking of their purpose. They were Catholics; they were working for foreign missions; they were a society; they were Americans. They left out no word except *North* before *America*. They had to have it grand in order that it might be explicit. But the name represented as yet no visible grandeur, not even when they enlisted a third priest to stand with them, Father John I. Lane, the suffering priest who acted as chaplain of the Daly Industrial School. They were three men, surely enough, but they were three men without a roof. They were a seminary without students, without an endowment, and even without teachers. They were merely a name, with a magazine, *The Field Afar*, which did not need the name.

They wanted to justify the title as soon as possible: they wished to be real. They wanted to begin. And in order to have a beginning, it was necessary to have a place on the map. The Boston office of *The Field Afar* would not do. In spite of the cordiality of Archbishop O'Connell of Boston, it was not considered that Boston was central enough for a national seminary. The phrase, "of America," in their title, suggested headquarters more centrally placed in America. Some counselors suggested Washington and the Catholic University as central, but was Washington central in relation to the Catholic population of the United States? Bishop Michael J. Hoban of Scranton, Pennsylvania, was a bishop with a missionary spirit, and he offered them a site, and he was more centrally placed, but Scranton was not a nationally known name. New York City was certainly not geographically central, but it was central in regard to the greatest hive of Catholic population in the United States. Within a four-hundred-mile radius of New York City lived seven and one-half million Catholics, well over a third of all those in the entire country. Archbishop Farley of New York offered the three priests a harborage in his diocese, and they accepted it.

New York City itself was out of the question. There was no corner of New York where a seminary could live placidly, and have a garden with turnips in it, in which to have processions on Rogation Days, as did the seminary in Paris on the corner of the *Rue Babylone* and the *Rue du Bac*. Land in New York was too precious, and buildings there, in order to be capacious, had to extend upwards to the moon. But outside of New York, twenty miles or so, the countryside could be as drowsy as any countryside. In Westchester County, east of the shining street of the Hudson River, twenty-nine miles north of Broadway, lay a village known as Hawthorne, not far from Washington Irving's Sleepy Hollow. It already had a special Catholic history. A daughter of the novelist Hawthorne, turned Catholic, and dedicated as a Sister of Saint Dominic, had there established a Cancer Hospital. Hence the very name "Hawthorne." And some French Dominicans, exiles from anticlerical France, had there found a refuge under an ex-missioner from Tonkin, Père Cothonay. Also near there was a house of the Salesian Fathers, which might be for sale, and might make a future mission seminary. Father Walsh decided that the temporary site of the Catholic Foreign Mission Seminary of America could well be in Hawthorne.

On October 20, 1911, Fathers Walsh and Price arrived at Hawthorne to stay as guests with the Dominicans. They found themselves perched on a hill in a region which was all hills. If there was a flat field in Hawthorne, they could not see it. And all the hundred little hills of Hawthorne were covered with trees turned gold and autumnal. As the leaves fell, they could see farther and farther to other hilltops about them, and they peered this way and that way, looking for a roof which they could make their own. The hospitable Dominicans said that they might as well continue with them, and needed no other roof. But there was no place for Father Lane among the Dominicans, and, since he was extremely anxious to give his help to the founders, they had to find a place for three rather than for two. And furthermore, to continue as guests of the Dominicans was for them what it was for newly married to continue in a mother-in-law's house: the putting off of some troubles, but also the indefinite postponement of independence. The leaves fell off the trees, but did not disclose a house that was neither too big nor too small, nor too near nor too far, and yet was for sale or for rent.

On the other hand, a cottage was found which could house their secretaries. It will be remembered that various young women had come to the help of Father Walsh in his editing of *The Field Afar,* conspicuous among them Miss Mary Rogers. They were indispensable to the running of that periodical, and were needed at Hawthorne if the periodical were to be edited at Hawthorne, as it was. Some of them held positions in Boston which they could not immediately leave. Miss Rogers, for instance, was teaching in that city in the public schools. But three of them were free to come immediately, and eager to come. One of these was Mary Louise Wholean, a recent graduate of Wellesley College; another was Sara Sullivan, an erstwhile secretary at the Harvard Medical School; the third was Mary Dwyer. A house near the Dominicans, and near the hospital of the Dominican Sisters, at which they could attend Mass, was accordingly hired. Other rooms under another roof were found for them as their office rooms. This meant that they would have no difficulty in taking the air as they went from devotion to work and from work to rest. They would have to be good walkers, even good mountain climbers. But the prospect did not frighten them. They arrived when the air had become nipping cold, and the paths had become slippery with ice and drifts of snow. The date of their arrival was January 6, the Feast of the Epiphany, when the Magi had arrived at Our Lord's cradle. Father Cothonay, admiring their wisdom and masculine courage, could only hail them as "The Three Wise Women."

Finally a house was found for the men, for the three of them. It was visible in winter from the Dominicans', but so far away over hills and valleys that it looked as if it were in another State of the Union. It was a cottage perched on a slope down which one could involuntarily ski even without skis when there was snow. When there was no snow, when there had come a thaw, the slope was made of a gluey clay in which Father Walsh was to learn how easy it was to lose his rubbers when he waded to the railroad station. The house was known as the Klinger Cottage, and one of its advantages was that it had a room which had been used by the French Dominicans for a chapel, and could be so used again. It had no electric light; there was no public water supply. Yet it had a well, and pipes for running water if the water were pumped. And it had a hot-water steam furnace. It was a perfectly habitable house. The three Fathers moved into this cottage on January 15.

There was nothing heroic about this occupation of Hawthorne. It was not a place of beyond-word hardships like the North Pole. Yet there was something very laughable about this self-imposed exile to it of the Catholic Foreign Mission Society of America. The "Three Wise Women" and the three priests had retreated to a location of perfect inconvenience so far as their functions were concerned.

The women could have better attended to *The Field Afar* in Boston, where it was being printed, and where its files and correspondence had stood in such good order. Moreover, at

Boston they would have had with them other secretaries who, although otherwise engaged during working hours, gave their off hours to *The Field Afar;* such as Miss Mary Rogers, who wanted to be with them yet could not—not till the school year should end.

The three men—Fathers Walsh, Price, and Lane—had no very obvious reason for wanting to live in a country village. They were not painters of winter landscapes. Father Walsh had often to be at Boston with the printer, and he had to be here and there at seminaries and colleges, inquiring about vocations. Father Price had by this time given away his *Truth* and did not have to bother with it; but he, too, had recruiting visits to make to colleges of his acquaintance, especially in Maryland and Pennsylvania. For neither of them was Hawthorne a particularly convenient railroad station, nor was the Klinger Cottage in Hawthorne one that they could easily leave to itself. Father Lane did not have affairs outside of Hawthorne; but, while he could regularly stay there, he could not stay there with any profit to his health, or with any manual competence. The Klinger Cottage was a less salubrious sanatorium for his rheumatism than had been the Daly Industrial School in Dorchester.

Yet the Catholic Foreign Mission Society had a determination that seemed quixotic. Men and women, they clung to Hawthorne as if God had given them sentinel duty there. The men were the more laughable, for they were the more helpless. They were no longer boys—the youngest of them was Father Walsh, forty-six—and they had, in entering the Klinger Cottage, wished on themselves the chores appropriate to laborers or young men. They had little money, and with it they could not hire a cook who would stay, and with it they chose, at first, not to afford the luxury of a chore man. Thus Father Walsh had to make himself cook; and Father Price, transplanted from a land where there were no furnaces, had to stoke a New York furnace; and Father Lane with a rheumatic arm had to wield a pump that was worse than rheumatic. They gave each other hardships. They were the subject for a comic supplement.

Almost within sight of the towering emporium of New York, choked with its supplies, they at times ran out of bread, and out of oil for the lamps. And the pump refused to give water. And the furnace refused to give heat. And the cooking was not always appetizing, or on time. This minor misery of want and ineptitude took place in sight of the city of American improvements, American world-known plumbing and competent quick-lunch counters.

Father Walsh used this situation, however, as a stepping-stone. It served to establish in this Catholic Foreign Mission Society of America a spirit of happy community, in which grandiloquence and pretense could not exist, in which little ironies could be faced with humility, and in which the sublimity of the work offered by God could not be obscured by any too-great show of mere human competence.

This spirit overflowed into *The Field Afar*. Father Walsh did not try to hide from its readers any of the grotesque difficulties. He made of them—he and Father Lane, who chronicled the laughable vicissitudes—a story which won the American confidence. Let us begin with the housekeeper or cook:

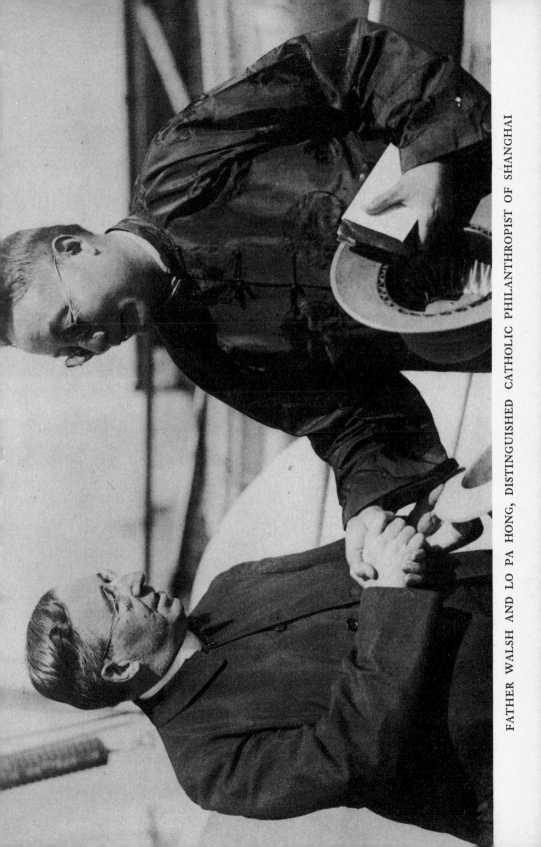

FATHER WALSH AND LO PA HONG, DISTINGUISHED CATHOLIC PHILANTHROPIST OF SHANGHAI

"A good-natured housekeeper, who had answered our advertisement, arrived in due time (she left after one week, but on excellent terms with us) and, after assurance from all sides, we found ourselves with no food, no oil (we like kerosene lamps), and *no* water. One disadvantage of the lack of water was that it affected rather seriously the life of a steam boiler, the pride of our cellar." [20]

Father Walsh had cooked for Father Stanton on Long Lake in the Adirondacks, but even at that:

"The hitch comes when there is no one to pour water into the kettle and watch it boil—to peel, or at least to wash, the jacketed potatoes—to keep stray cats away from the larder." [21]

Father Lane did not belittle his trials with the water supply:

"Thursday, February 1, 1912. Today both Fathers spoke to me about Holy Water. Rather, Father Walsh spoke last night, and at noon Father Price said, 'Here we have been in the house for two weeks and not a drop of Holy Water.' Father Lane responded: 'Wait until we get water first. No one can bless what he has not got.' And it is true. At the time Father Lane thought of blessing the water, there was no water. Water is a most precious article around here. Many mornings we have to be contented with a dry wash. And for decency's sake get a few drips somewhere before the beginning of the Holy Sacrifice, to wash the fingers." [22]

Ten days later there was a new housekeeper, and water was flowing in the Klinger Cottage. But now, though there was not too much housekeeper, there was too much water. It had taken to leaking through the house in an unholy manner.

"Sunday, February 11, 1912. Just as we were preparing to

retire, another leak was discovered in the bathroom, from the overflow of the tank this time, so that we went upstairs and prepared to empty the tank. We scooped out all the water we could, in as many empty vessels as were on hand. Then forming a line, Father Walsh, Father Lane, and the housekeeper passed vessels to each other and emptied the water out of Father Price's room. Then we found the stopper, which could have done the business at the start! There is no doubt but that we are learning." [23]

All the clergy were in favor of the intentions of these exiles in Hawthorne. Not all were impressed by their competence, and some held that, even if competent, they were trying for what was impossible. Of the Catholic periodicals, the only one which spoke of their enterprise with optimism was the Hartford *Catholic Transcript,* edited by Father Walsh's classmate, Monsignor Duggan. But Father Walsh was not in the least discouraged. His own feats in cooking might be laughable, but God's work was not. And God's work was going on in spite of mistakes, and there would some day be a real seminary and real seminarians. The one great need was to pray enough.

One winter afternoon he called at Cathedral College in New York City. The college was under the charge of Archbishop Farley, who knew Father Walsh very well. It was the preparatory school of the archdiocesan seminary, Saint Joseph's at Dunwoodie. But Father Walsh was far from being a celebrity whom the students knew. He inquired of a student if the Rector, Monsignor Hayes, were at hand. Gone. And what was the Father's name? Father Walsh. (Oh, another Father Walsh.) And what did the Father want? He had something to do with foreign missions, and wondered what students might be interested. The student was sorry that no one was around. It was indeed late in the day.

"But I have a friend who is daft on foreign missions," suddenly remembered the student. "He will want to see you. He is in the library."

Then he went off to find his friend. No, he was not there—must have gone. "Good night, Father."

A second later the friend turned up. "What! a priest here who was starting a seminary for foreign missions? I will run after him. Which way?"

The friend's name was Francis X. Ford. He came from Brooklyn, but it was on Madison Avenue that he overtook Father James Anthony Walsh, once of Boston, now wintering at Hawthorne on the Hudson. Then and there Francis X. Ford registered himself as the first seminarian of the Catholic Foreign Mission Society of America.

Before the first of February, Father Walsh had received thirty-five letters inquiring about the possibility of entering his seminary. It was gratifying that twenty-one came from Massachusetts, his own State, for prophets are often not honored at home. It was assuring that five came from New York, into which he had immigrated. It was surprising that one came from Missouri, and one from Panama. Later on he was to learn from a Chinese merchant, a convert, that, in a world made by God, the only surprising thing is that anyone should be surprised. But what were letters?

In Maryland, meanwhile, there lived a lad, native of Cumberland, who had passed through Mount Saint Mary's College at Emmitsburg as a lay student with the intention of continuing in a lay career: James E. Walsh. He was now working in a steel company. But he was a religious layman, and one day he read a copy of the Boston publication, *The Field Afar*. The thought came to his mind: "I might be a foreign missioner." During the winter Father Price visited his region. He met Father Price, and before they parted he, too, had signed up. Why be surprised?

Before April arrived, there were six future students assured to the seminary. But where was the seminary?

The Klinger Cottage had passed through the winter, like a ship repaired in midocean!

"Our shell of a cottage, where frosted windows during the winter used to shake like an old man's teeth, laughing at our discomfort, looks positively picturesque and restful."[24]

It was even being properly manned. It had early appeared that a band of lay Brothers was needed to relieve the Fathers of duties for which they were unfitted. Such had been prayed for; and such had arrived in the person of Ernst Höllger, an Austrian, and Thomas McCann, a Brooklynite with the most Brooklyn accent in Brooklyn, who could sing like an angel.

But the Klinger Cottage could never serve as a seminary. Never did the Fathers write on their letterheads, "The Klinger Cottage, Hawthorne, N. Y." Instead they gave their address as "Maryknoll"—a name composed of Our Lady's name and the title "Knoll" which had become dear to Father Walsh from his having spent vacations at a place called "The Knolls." But Maryknoll continued to be a land of nowhere. This fact had to be explained in *The Field Afar:*

"Maryknoll is not our Post Office. It is rather a title of a dream which we hope will, before long, be realized.

"Maryknoll will, to speak more clearly, be the name of the knoll on which we will locate permanently our seminary building." [25]

Before April was over, Father Walsh was ready to buy a piece of land that could be called Maryknoll. He had been named Superior of his Society. Also the Society had assumed legal status. Under the laws of the State of New York it was duly incorporated on April 30, the members of its corporation being His Eminence, Cardinal Farley; Monsignor Patrick J. Hayes (then President of Cathedral College and later to be himself Cardinal Archbishop of New York); Monsignor John J. Dunn, Director in New York of the Society for the Propagation of the Faith; Honorable Victor J. Dowling, Justice of the Appellate Division of New York; Major John F. O'Rourke; and Michael Maginnis. Financially Father Walsh had been tided over the winter mostly by his Boston friends in the priesthood, but partly by new friends in New York City, notably Miss Julia Ward. Cardinal Farley had endowed a burse for the education of some future seminarian. Gifts had been collected. But where was there land to buy?

Westchester County still seemed to be the best location. In it were the Dominicans, who could serve as teachers of the seminary. And then there was Dunwoodie Seminary several miles off, at which his students could receive instruction. But where was there a place near Hawthorne and near Dunwoodie? Thoughts of buying a house belonging to the Salesians had been dropped.

May 20 was the anniversary of Father Walsh's ordination, a day on which to celebrate and congratulate one's self and do no work. This year he worked. It was not repairing pipes. It was not writing a book. It was using his eyes, peering here and there on the slopes east of the Hudson River, looking for his house and his lot of land. In the evening he found that he had been unsuccessful, yet he refused to be disturbed. He wrote a letter to Margaret Hughes, the daughter of his sister, Mrs. Thomas B. Hughes:

"I thought you might like to read a letter from your old uncle who has been trying to learn again, after some years, the typewriter.

"I spent a happy anniversary of my ordination, but was away most of the day looking up land so as to get as soon as possible a home of our own that will be bigger than your doll house.

"We are quite comfortable and happy here now. The birds are making us light-hearted, the lilacs light-headed, and the view from the piazza is fine. We sit out after every meal for our recreation (a big word), and after the Hudson River boat has gone by, we start night prayers. The boat is five miles away, but it throws a light over the hills around us.

"Watch the improvement in my next letter!"

On July 10 it seemed that a habitation had been found: a long, low, two-story house, overlooking the Hudson River, with fifty-two acres of land. And it could be called a knoll, for it was among hills, the Pocantico Hills. And it had the advantage of being not five miles from Hawthorne and near a novitiate of the Christian Brothers. And it

had a wonderful spring on the property, which laughed at
their former troubles with a pump. Here was a dream come
true, a prayer answered, a proof of God's loving Providence
taking tender care of them.

But the omnipotent Mr. John D. Rockefeller, who neigh-
bored this property, was permitted by God to put an end to
this dream. Even though Father Walsh had clinched the
purchase by the payment of ten thousand dollars, Mr. Rockefeller, or his agent, catching news of the prospective transac-
tion and thinking that one public institution—the novitiate of
the Christian Brothers—was enough in his vicinity, stepped in
with limitless wealth and bought the land. Mr. Rockefeller
professed to have been unaware that the ten thousand had
been paid by Father Walsh, and finally, after several lawsuits,
offered the Society eight thousand dollars in damages. This
was a happy contribution to a good cause, and probably did
the Society, taking all in all, a good turn. But in July, 1912,
it left Father Walsh in distress.

On August 10 he was still without a Maryknoll. That date
was the Feast of Saint Lawrence, and he happened to have a
relic of Saint Lawrence. This he set by the tabernacle of the
altar in the Klinger Cottage. "Give us a Maryknoll."

Four days later, the eve of the Feast of the Assumption,
he happened upon a farm on a hill on the outskirts of Ossining. The hill was called in Ossining "Sunset Hill." It looked
to China, and between it and China lay the Tappan Zee, made
by the widening of the Hudson River. It consisted of ninety-
three acres, woodland and tillage. It had three houses and a
barn. It was thirty-four miles from New York City, and six

from Hawthorne. It was for sale, and could be bought for less than the Pocantico property—which was nearer to New York—would have cost: even for $44,500. Father Walsh set his heart on it.

On August 18 he bought the property. In fear that, if a priest approached the proprietor, the proprietor might balk, he had presented Miss Mary Rogers as the prospective purchaser. Together with two real-estate agents, he had accompanied her as chauffeur in a linen duster and goggles, worn in those dusty days by automobilists. The property was deeded to Miss Mary Rogers; and then, on that same evening, for one dollar was deeded to his Society. It was the octave day of Saint Lawrence.

On September 9 a load of furniture, horse-drawn, trundled from the Klinger Cottage to Sunset Hill. On September 18 a cab drew up at the Klinger Cottage. Into it crowded all those of the Catholic Foreign Mission Society of America who were present then at the Klinger Cottage. First there was one of the Society's two founders, Father Walsh. Father Price, the other founder, had not yet returned from another visit to Lourdes, in France. Then there were three students, who had inhabited the Klinger Cottage for four days: they were Francis Xavier Ford, of Brooklyn; James Edward Walsh, of Cumberland, Maryland; and William Francis O'Shea, of Hoboken, New Jersey. Then there were two lay Brothers. And the seventh was the driver.

The cab began to move in the direction of the Hudson River in the September twilight, like a caricature carriage in a black-and-white etching by Daumier. It moved jerkily behind a lame horse, to which the creaking axles chirruped. Father Walsh has described the scene with more courtesy to the vehicle than I may seem to be giving:

"It was a raw evening when we left Hawthorne, under cover of darkness, so as to spare the feelings of the villagers. We had six miles to drive; and, into a carriage built for four, seven of us crowded—just as our ancestors used to do that they might give decent burial to their devoted friends. We, however, were attending a resurrection, not a funeral; and as we clung to some oil lamps that were to give us the first heat and light in our new home, our hearts were glad." [26]

They were hungry by the time they arrived at Sunset Hill, and the sunset was gone. They entered a farmhouse, the main farmhouse of the estate they had bought, which they were calling already "Maryknoll! Maryknoll!" They feasted therein on "soused herring" and bad coffee. Lanterns began to go about the rooms. Where, by the way, was the altar stone, which they had brought so carefully with them? But, wherever it was, this was Maryknoll.

"Hawthorne," they said, "was our Bethlehem. Sunset Hill is our Nazareth."

The Trainer

How LONG seems the training for anything, a battle or a game! At first it is long because one is not accustomed to it; then it is long because one is so accustomed to it that one cannot imagine its end.

Maryknoll now became a training place for foreign missioners. The course of training at the seminary would regularly last six years. As it happened, there were several of the students who had by previous schooling anticipated some of that training and might be ready to become missioners in four. But the first real rank of missioners would not be ready until six years had passed; and, since it was now the fall of 1912, that would not be until 1918. Not until 1918 would action begin. Six years, seen already in the future, seem interminable. Six years, seen from any direction by a human eye, are a long time. These particular six years were to seem especially long because outward events were to move so fast in them. They were to be filled with the whirl and tumult and fast heartbeat of the First World War. They were to be a time when all inaction seemed long, because the attention of all men was turned upon action. Mere student life in the hallucination of the day seemed one of a whole lifetime. Maryknoll was starting on six long years.

Even the first twenty-four hours of Maryknoll were a long twenty-four hours, and as bewildering as a recruit's first day in the army. We remember that lights had been going about the house on the evening of the eighteenth of September, 1912, looking for the altar stone for the Mass to be said on the next morning. Early the next morning eyes were still looking for the same stone, but it could not be found. Yet there must be Mass. So the Catholic Foreign Mission Society of America trooped at daybreak a mile and more to the town of Ossining, level with the Hudson River, where the parish priest, the Reverend Doctor Mahoney, lent them the convent chapel.

On the return journey one thing was certain: the troop was hungry for breakfast, and would have a good breakfast, for a reliable woman had been engaged as cook and must now be busy in the kitchen. On arriving once again on the summit of Sunset Hill, the troop entered the farmhouse, famished and trying not to push, and found an empty breakfast table, and a fireless stove, on which had been laid chillily a note with pencilings on it—a poem from the cook. The words were unrhymed but they were Shakespearian: she had been frightened by the silence and had fled.

At this the "rich lady" who had bought the farm and sold it to the Society for one dollar, Miss Rogers, once of Smith College, was sent for from Hawthorne. She arrived, not only by herself but with a less timid cousin of the departed cook, and earned for herself one of her many titles to being called a founder of Maryknoll by cooking Maryknoll's first really hot and homelike meal.

Two days later arrived the three other students: William E. Lambert, of Buffalo, New York; Alphonse S. Vogel, of New York City; and Daniel L. McShane, of Columbus, Indiana. Immediately there began as initiation to the Seminary a week's retreat. Father Walsh was the retreat master, with Father Lane, who had now arrived, helping him. The reader does not have to be told what Father Walsh said, for he said what all his life up till then he had been saying. It concerned not merely the nature of a missionary vocation, but the way of being a Christian, particularly a Christian in a religious community. "To those who love God, all things work together for good." Also a saying of Cardinal Vaughan's was cited: "In working for God, it matters little who does the work, provided the work be done."

Father Walsh had a sense of humor, and he was aware as well as any mischievous student might be that this latter maxim had an equivocal meaning. It really meant that it mattered not at all who got the external credit for a deed. It could be twisted to mean that one could let another do his work for him. But in spite of this danger lurking in the phraseology, he clung to it as stating fundamentally what must be the spirit of Maryknoll, and it still hangs placarded in Maryknoll's corridors. Maryknollers were not to go about smiling at the feats they had personally performed. They were to be as selfless as children sometimes, to grown-ups, appear to be. And they were to be as joyous as proverbial children, and yet not lifted up with joy's emotion. Their joy was to be tempered with restraint—"for excess in anything always brings its unwholesome reactions."

On the last day of the retreat, the Feast of Saint Michael, Father "Bernadette" Price arrived from Lourdes, his own face a final sermon.

There still continued to be homely material difficulties—an echo of days at Hawthorne. Water had to be carried from a "field afar." But, before October was well on, electricity had arrived, which gave a chance to use a gasoline pump, and the Society began to boast of its conveniences.

"With our electric power comes the opportunity to use electric light when necessary. . . . Water, light, telephone, bread (it took us some time to find a baker whose horse would climb to see us), the assurance of a coal supply (not so easy), an accessible Armour cooler, a refrigerator of our own, large enough for a side of any old thing with four legs, a live horse, 'Billy,' who can walk more rapidly than he can run, but who never shies at a hill, a four-seated wagon (it cost $15) for the use of live or dead meat, a truncated 'Little Sisters of the Poor' conveyance, a dog whose fourth leg goes bad occasionally but whose night bark never fails, and a small army of hens—these are actualities." [27]

Also in the happy month of October with its gilded leaves, one of the other farmhouses was vacated by a tenant farmer, and became "Saint Michael's," or the headquarters of the auxiliary laymen, who were now a busy three. Into another cottage, on October 15, moved the secretaries, who still, in the occasional absence of cooks, had to take care of the nourishment of the helpless sex, besides attending to the secretarial work connected with *The Field Afar,* which now had twelve thousand subscribers. October 15 was the Feast of Saint Teresa of Avila, and the secretaries' cottage became "Saint Teresa's Lodge."

November 21 was also an important date. In the Church calendar, November 21 is the Feast of the Presentation of Our Blessed Mother. In the calendar of the Sulpicians—and it was by Sulpicians that Father Walsh had been trained for the priesthood—it was a day hallowed for the renewal of clerical promises. In the calendar of Father Walsh's heart, it was the earthly birthday of Blessed Théophane Vénard, who, as cheerful missioner and cheerful martyr, was an example to the members of Father Walsh's new Society, and was also the Society's special chosen patron. On this day "the little Seminary chapel at Maryknoll"—so wrote Father Walsh in his *Field Afar*— "was the scene of an interesting and impressive ceremony on the Feast of the Presentation of the Blessed Virgin Mary, when our first students, six in number, were invested with cassock and cincture." On this day, too, there descended on the community, so averred Father Walsh, who was loath to be sentimental, "a joyous restraint, and peace born of common desire to sacrifice all for God." [28]

At the beginning of the new year, 1913, Father Walsh was able to send an assuring report to the Sacred Congregation of Propaganda:

"1. We have a permanent location, excellent and quite ample in view of further development.

"2. On the property, which cost us (for 93 acres of land and all buildings) $44,500, we have paid $15,000, leaving a mortgage of $30,000, which we shall be free and, we believe, prepared to cancel in three years.

"3. Our official organ, *The Field Afar,* has proved profitable, not only as a direct investment, but indirectly by securing for us a steady stream of gifts.

"4. The work has been welcomed by a very satisfactory proportion of the bishops, priests, and laity throughout the country, and new friends are being added daily to our lists.

"5. We have reason to believe that within a year we shall be in possession of at least twelve foundations ($5,000 each); and we shall have accumulated, in addition, a substantial portion of the full amount necessary to pay for our property, besides, meeting all current expenses. We have already three complete burses, including one from His Eminence, Cardinal Farley, who has shown his constant interest in our work.

"6. Finally, in view of the number of students (six), with whom we begin, and of the encouragement given by religious teachers in various parts of the country, we have the strong hope of a steady flow of excellent vocations." [29]

On the same first of January, 1913, *The Field Afar* celebrated its seventh birthday. It had come to the age of reason. It would from now on appear monthly.

February 22 was another birthday anniversary: George Washington's Birthday. And on the twenty-third Father Walsh's birthday was celebrated. It is true that Father Walsh had been born on February 24; but, since he was booked to go on the twenty-fourth to the hospital for a slight operation on his nose, the community anticipated his birthday to surprise him. Daniel McShane, the senior of the students, delivered an address, not extemporaneous, but in student manner learned by heart and yet not thoroughly learned, in which he praised Father Walsh as founder of this new project which was going on so happily for all. Father Walsh in response reminded him that Father Price, at that moment absent on a recruiting tour, was just as much a founder. Father Price was the "Mary," he was only the "Martha."

Then came the spring, and it confronted Father Walsh with a new, unfaced responsibility. He was the "Martha" of Maryknoll, but Maryknoll happened to be not only a Seminary, it was a farm.

"In our boyhood," he said, speaking with a mock-heroic, grandiose *we,* "we had many ambitions, running from the swinging seat of a coal driver to the presidential chair, but, as far as we can recall, we never dared aspire to the independence of farm life. Yet here we have been buying horses, pigs, hens, a plow, a sprayer, seeds, and sundry other things that made the first of May a day of dreadful reckoning from which we have not yet recovered.

"We had an early planting after April Fools' Day. It was a horse, a promising animal, gray and mighty, with a fine chance for development between his ribs. Meningitis carried him off, and he lies in 'a little dust quiescent,' at a safe distance from the barn that sheltered him. . . ."

Another horse was purchased, but the newcomer had ideas of his own. "He rested well after his labors but insisted on having breakfast in bed the next morning, and refused to get up until Angelo approached with a crowbar. Then, quite unassisted, our weary 'Harry' shifted his legs to the perpendicular

CURIOUS CHINESE GATHER ABOUT FATHER WALSH AS
HE ATTEMPTS TO RECITE HIS BREVIARY ON THE SHIP'S
DECK

and walked out of his comfortable box-stall without a crutch. He has been quite well ever since." [30]

Father Walsh did know the fundamentals of farming life. The fields, as well as his addressing machines and his typewriters and his school desks, belonged to God. On April 27 he had a procession and a blessing of the fields for Rogation Sunday, as the Paris seminarians had in their hidden yet spacious garden on the *Rue du Bac*—one of the beautiful, unexpected, hidden things of citified Paris. And he asked prayers for his crops from readers of *The Field Afar*.

"So, dear reader, when in your litany you pray for the preservation of the fruits of the earth, remember the farm at Maryknoll, and have pity on those of us who are so unfortunate as to have walked in our youth on bricks, rather than on green and grassy carpets covered with daisies and dandelions." [31]

Yet by his respect for human experience he was aware that at forty-six years of age he could not himself become a magisterial farmer—not even with faithful Auxiliaries of Saint Michael to help him. Therefore he hired a real farmer to farm for him. He was learning what he could do and what he could not do. So was each of his students.

As soon as the first year was over, as soon as the seasons had shown all their surprises, Maryknoll began to settle down to the somewhat repetitive life of a seminary. In one respect the second year was almost too much like the first. In September, 1913, the Seminary of Sunset Hill began again its studies with the same number of students as before—six—and the six were the identical same, with their cassocks one year older. This was not so much a failure in recruitment as an accident in the manner in which the recruitment came. An apostolic school, or preparatory seminary, The Vénard, had, through the generosity of Bishop Hoban of Scranton, been started in his diocese, and at it there were eight new Maryknollers; but they were not at Sunset Hill, and they were not directly under Father Walsh's care, for at The Vénard Father Lane had been set in charge.

It was not entirely encouraging to begin a second year at Maryknoll with no sign of increase, but it did give the original six of Maryknoll a chance to weld themselves into a unit. It gave the teachers a chance to correct any first mistakes they might have made, and to have a second start. The first year was something like a trial turn of the course. The second year was almost the first real year.

On this second round of the seasons, the six students had the calm of veterans. September, 1913, began with a retreat given by the Redemptorist, Father Henry Borgmann, who was one of the special friends of Maryknoll, so familiar to the original six students that he was called "Uncle Henry." At the end of the retreat, during the Solemn High Mass, a cloudburst came in the sky, and the not-quite-finished roof of the temporary chapel was not ready to keep out the deluge. Two important leaks sprinkled their shower bath, one on the organ, which hissed and died like a drowning man, and the other on the preaching Father Borgmann. The six were now like veterans under fire. They took it with unconcern, without turning their heads in their ranks. They had become used to such normal Maryknoll vicissitudes.

The first year's training at Maryknoll had gone on somewhat by improvisation. There was not a full faculty, and there was no previous experience to which to look back. The aim had been first of all to provide an instruction similar to that received in ordinary diocesan seminaries.

The students were divided, as at usual seminaries, into those less advanced, who were referred to as "philosophers," and those nearer ordination, who were "theologians." To begin with, the only theologians were James E. Walsh, and Daniel McShane, and, since there was no theological faculty at Maryknoll, they had been forced to commute to Dunwoodie, until in the spring of 1913 the Dominicans from Hawthorne had begun to supply a theological faculty in the person of Father William Owens, O.P. The rest of the instruction consisted of a special weekly course in Advanced English, taught by Father Walsh; and of regular courses such as Holy Scripture, which was given the first year by Father McCabe, who had been lent to Maryknoll by Mill Hill in England, and Ecclesiastical History, which was taught by Father Lane, and Philosophy, which was taught by the Reverend Placido Barile, a priest from Rome.

But there was also a special instruction due to future missioners that was not necessary for diocesan priests. Father Lane, for instance, gave a course in Chinese History, and Father McCabe gave lessons in manual training. Occasionally the seminarians visited Sing Sing Prison, in Ossining, at the invitation of its ideal chaplain, Father Cashin, there to give instructions—not that the pagans they would later instruct were criminals, but it was well to be adaptable. Then there was Doctor Paluel Flagg, who gave them hints in Medical First Aid.

But even more important than a slightly different curriculum, was the different spiritual and moral training. Certain qualities were especially necessary to missioners—rather unbookish qualities. They would be far from bishops to obey, far from carpenters and plumbers to command. They should be men of action, quick to decide, hardy, versatile. They were trained to walk the earth and to act with practicality.

"A stranger coming to Maryknoll," wrote Father Walsh, "need not be surprised to meet one of the seminarians in overalls, working on the grounds, or clad in apron, scrubbing the floor within the house. These duties have been carried out, we are glad to say, not in the camp-life spirit, which accepts them as recreative and passing, but seriously and naturally, as part of the training for a soldier of Christ." [32]

During the second year the instruction went on with a new firmness and with that happy monotony which is necessary to all real training. The only disquietudes were those of the Superior, who had to provide the money to see that the training could go on. Father Walsh refused to let financial anxieties bother his peace of mind, and he certainly never bothered the students with mention of them. But after the various crises had passed, he did regale the readers of *The Field Afar* with an account of them. Readers should be reminded that a seminary could not live on air. Men were not angels, bodiless. It was for the friends of Maryknoll to play their foreign-missionary part by supplying the funds to feed and house and prepare missioners.

Once it had been his policy, while beginning at the S. P. F. in Boston, to ask for only cents or "crumbs." He had learned from experience to ask boldly for what he needed—dollars and tens of dollars. In the December, 1913, number of *The Field Afar* Father Walsh gave a hint of his recurring financial stringencies, and gave it cheerfully yet unforgettably:

"We needed it badly—you know what. And we were wondering from what point of the compass it would come and through what providential instrument.

"The bank, or at least our corner of it, had just been drained, and we were looking forward to a call on that corner for two thousand dollars plus a few hundred more.

"We were doing our best and had no time to do more. So we weren't worrying. But it did feel good, one frosty morning, to open a letter and find within it a check for $2,750.

"The bulk of this amount was expected, but it came sooner than we anticipated, and with a gratifying addition. It represented the residue of the modest estate of a priest of Salem, Massachusetts, the Reverend Timothy T. Murphy, who died two years ago.

"May the Master of the Apostles reward this generous and thoughtful benefaction! We ask our readers to give Father Murphy, in gratitude for his service to our Cause, at least a passing prayer. We will do more.

"The tide was low again, November 12. Contractors don't wait till the product is finished before clamoring for the wherewithal, and a requisition was due, which, added to other obligations, threatened to leave us in some dark clam hole.

"We had faced a similar crisis three weeks before and had

been unexpectedly saved. This time the amount required was not so great, and five hundred good dollars more than we could scrape together would meet our need. So we smiled out Mr. Contractor with the assurance of a fair proportion, to be followed by the balance.

"Just as he left, a carriage drew up at one of our doors (we don't know which is the front of the house yet). The visitors were two priests: one the prison chaplain (Father Cashin), the other a much-loved New York pastor, whose charity to the unfortunate is known throughout the country.

"We are always glad to receive our priests, but this was the visit of a rather portly angel who had just been made beneficiary under a poor woman's will and had come to turn her nest egg of several hundred dollars over to us. The tide had turned in our favor.

"The next mail brought an anonymous gift of one hundred dollars under the postmark, *Boston*." [33]

So the training did go on. And in June, 1914, there was a new wooden chapel annexed to the pro-Seminary, with an altar in it presented by Miss Julia Ward of New York. On June 22 Bishop Cusack, Auxiliary of New York, dedicated it, and on the same day Daniel McShane was raised to the subdiaconate.

Then came August, 1914, when began the World War. This had repercussions on little, apparently isolated, Maryknoll. Father McCabe was called back to Mill Hill and sent to Africa, where a special need for missioners was created by the internment in English possessions of missioners of German nationality. From China three hundred French missioners were called back to France to serve in the French army. This left gaps in the missionary ranks in China, for the filling of which Rome looked hopefully to the United States, and to Maryknoll.

Maryknoll in the fall of 1914 did give Rome some reason for hopefulness. At its center on the Hudson it had twice as many students as it had had for the first two years, even thirteen. At its preparatory seminary, The Vénard, it had twelve. These enrollments were not enormous, but they showed a sudden increase which made it difficult for the Catholic Foreign Mission Society, with its large name and small resources, to find for them teachers. Once again the Dominicans of Hawthorne came to their help. First Father Owens, O.P., was joined by Father Hyacinth Foster, O.P.; and then both, in 1915, were succeeded by a twain who were to give the greater part of their lives to Maryknoll, Fathers John A. McHugh, O.P., and Charles J. Callan, O.P. Also the services of a remarkably scholarly parish pastor, Doctor Thomas P. Phelan, of Brewster, New York, were secured.

Even then the teaching staff was so shorthanded that, when Father Lane's health gave out at The Vénard, there was no priest to put in his place, and Daniel McShane, still only a deacon, had to be set in charge. Rome might be looking to Maryknoll hopefully; China might be looking to Maryknoll hopefully; but there must be four winters more before the training of a real mission band could be completed.

On November 10, 1914, Daniel McShane was ordained priest in Saint Patrick's Cathedral, New York, Cardinal Farley officiating. After the ordination the Cardinal said to the young levite:

"It has been a pleasant duty for me to ordain the first priest for Maryknoll. You are privileged to be the first one. Many will follow you. So lead, that these many may see the way clear to follow after you, up, up to the very throne of God. May God bless you!" [34]

Father Walsh commented in the *Maryknoll Chronicle*: "War news brings daily accounts of a depleted mission force in the Far East, and of empty seminaries in Europe. Will America rise to the emergency and fill the gap in Christ's army beyond the frontier?" [35]

For a moment he entertained the idea of sending over Father McShane alone, as a lone American missioner to be brigaded with the French of the Paris Foreign Mission Society. But no. Haste would be waste. There should be a real Maryknoll contingent representing the United States, or nothing. There were now thirteen future missioners at Maryknoll, and twelve younger ones at Scranton. There would in time be a Maryknoll expeditionary force.

In 1915 Rome, through Cardinal Gotti, sent them a message of encouragement, a *Decretum Laudis,* which, though formal in its language and concerned specifically with approving the provisional statutes of organization which had been adopted by the Society, yet referred significantly to the "very enterprising people of the United States," and announced that "Our Most Holy Father, Pope Benedict XV," had placed the Society under the immediate jurisdiction of "this Sacred Congregation of *Propaganda Fide.*" Thus in 1915, four years after the Society's foundation, came the Holy See's first formal word of praise.

A year and a half later, "the enterprising people of the United States of North America" entered the World War— on April 6, 1917. The Catholic Foreign Mission Society of that "enterprising people" was then five years old. It had—counting the ordinations of June, 1917—ten priests in its personnel, and sixty students, twenty-five of them at Sunset Hill, besides a dozen Auxiliaries, and forty thousand subscribers to *The Field Afar*. It was almost ready to begin its "world war."

Before it sent missioners into the field of battle—which was not in Europe, but in the East, towards which the eyes of the public were not looking—Father Walsh determined to make an exploring trip. He had a double reason for making it. He wished to know what the field of battle was really like, and where, if anywhere, those in charge would give his platoon a place at the front.

From letters and books, and also from listening to private reminiscences of missioners, he knew a great deal about mission conditions in the Orient. But his very practical mind could learn best when it was on the spot, where his eyes could see, his ears hear, and his feet feel. Then, and then only, could he know the situation foursquare, and feel the intuitions shot through his brain. Then he could make his best judgments. He needed to set foot in the East.

For years he had been receiving congratulations from the East, with hints that almost anywhere his men might be needed. But he understood enough of vague compliments to be aware that they are no more to be trusted than anything else vague. Five years earlier, at the very founding of Mary-knoll, Bishop Merel of Canton had definitely promised to give him some day a field in his province, but just when was "some day?" And did a promise hold good after five years? Moreover, Bishop Merel had been succeeded in Canton by Bishop de Guébriant. This latter was personally known to Father Walsh. He had been met at the seminary in the *Rue du Bac,* and while still Vicar Apostolic of Szechwan had asked for reënforcements from Maryknoll. But now that he had been raised to Canton, mightn't he have changed his mind?

Father Walsh well knew that, under French courtesy, there was a certain lack of confidence in American Catholics as potential missioners. He was not at all sure that his men would easily obtain any opening. And he was not going to trust to courteous, formal letters to find that opening. He wanted to be on the spot, looking into the eyes of the giver of the compliments.

The Traveler

FATHER WALSH was a remarkable traveler. He was affable with fellow travelers, from whom he learned much, and to whom he often taught much. He was shrewd to observe the countries which he visited, and generous in his judgments of them. He was aware that, as a guest in the hands of an hospitable host, one can be shown only what is roseate. He accepted the courtesies of hospitality and saw through them, both to the kindness of heart that proffered them and to the human difficulties which they often hid. On the other hand, when the unseemly aspect of a new land showed itself first, he was not unduly impressed or depressed by its unseemliness. He expected good and bad, and was astute in being able to distinguish one from the other, being not one of those who are rigid in private or provincial prejudices. He could be most adroitly perceptive without appearing prying. Like a photographer—and he was also a photographer—he was expert at catching people off guard.

He crossed the continent in early September, 1917, picking up a prospective "vocation" in Colorado, and noting the ability of the Mormons in Utah making their propaganda, even as he sped by them. He arrived at San Francisco in time to open a Maryknoll halting place or "procure" there, at 1911 Van Ness Avenue. He listened to encouraging words from Archbishop Hanna.

Then he boarded, on September 15, 1917, a Japanese steamer, the *Tenyo Maru,* bound for Yokohama by way of a halt at Hawaii. On board with him was another Catholic priest, Father Chabloz, a Jesuit, French by birth, but the ship was no Catholic mission ship. It came nearer to being a Protestant one: there were twenty-five Protestant missionaries aboard, Americans from the United States.

It did not induce to self-complacency, this coming face to face with the superior missionary activity of Protestant fellow citizens. Neither was it soothing to hear the perfectly unguarded, friendly, frank comments of some of his Japanese and Chinese fellow passengers, as they stood beside him at the steamer rail.

"Ah, a Catholic priest," they would say to him, "and an American! Are there many of you in the United States? The Catholic Church does not count for much there, does it? The United States is Protestant. We think of Catholic priests as Europeans."

He stowed himself in a steamer chair and opened a little book of statistics, in order to strengthen his hopes and give himself less a sense of futility. And the ocean under him kept going up and down. The little book had been compiled by French Lazarists, followers of Saint Vincent de Paul, who in the United States were known as Vincentians. It gave him some data on both Catholic missions and Protestant missions in China. It read like this:

Catholic Missions in China

Catholics in China	1,729,323
Increase in one year	100,969
Priests—European	1,430
Priests—Native	575
Preparatory Students	1,887
Churches and Chapels	8,618

Protestant Missions in China

Societies	93
Missionaries—American and European	5,419
Missionaries—Native	17,879
Number of Stations	4,064
Total Number of Protestants	235,303 [36]

In these statistics there was one most striking fact: there were seven times as many Catholics as Protestants in China, even though there were but a fourth as many Catholic missioners as there were Protestants. This gave the impression that, for some reason, Catholic missioners were working more efficaciously. This awakened the hope that his missioners, the four or five that might cross the Pacific in the following year, would accomplish as much as these twenty-five Protestants on the *Tenyo Maru*.

Yet he knew that to arrive at such a conclusion was to make all sorts of leaps and bounds from shaky assumptions. And to begin with, the Catholic missioners who seemed to be doing so well with few numbers were, all of them, Europeans. Could American Catholic missioners do as well? He shut his eyes and looked into the far future. He knew they could. Then he opened his eyes, saw the immense sea again, and the steamer rail rising and falling, and at times with its rising cutting, in its slow slant, the steady horizon line. He saw the twenty-five Protestant missionaries trooping by.

He made friends with everyone. His mischievous lips, which did no mischief, and which were ready to smile, yet waited to come to Paradise before they fully smiled, did a little inadvertent instructing of the fellow passengers, acquainting them with the fact that there really were Catholics in the United States. He did not boast to the American Protestant missionaries that some day he would be sending more than twenty-five American Catholics across on some steamer as missioners. He did bring up the question with them of the good work that the European priests were doing. He showed them the statistics in his lap. Were they accurate? The Protestants did not know; they thought so.

But what are statistics? As soon as he should have crossed the Pacific, he could look beyond them. What are numbers? What are appearances? God has done inexplicable things with twelve men, with four men, even with one man—Saint Francis Xavier. The conquests of Saint Francis Xavier made those of Alexander the Great seem picayune.

But he must not dream, not even when he was praying to the Holy Spirit, the Dove of which was flying downward above his altar in Saint Paul's Chapel at Maryknoll. One thing was more than statistically certain. He would not find many American Catholic missioners anywhere on the other side of the Pacific. There were a few, enlisted in various orders such as the Franciscans, but they were looked on as Europeans and listed by the Vincentians as Europeans. They were both men and women. To those few he would pay special attention. But finding them would be as difficult as finding the first stars in an evening sky which was still blue.

Yokohama! It was October 3, 1917.

"At about 8 o'clock Wednesday morning, we passed through the breakwater and steamed slowly up to the dock. A haze was over Yokohama, and the first glimpse of the Japanese city was not inspiring. It looked too modern at that distance to be very interesting, except for the consciousness that we were actually about to enter Japan.

"We had said Masses at an early hour on the boat. Father Chabloz, loyal Jesuit that he is, offered the Mass of Saint Francis Xavier; and I, as a professedly world-wide Catholic, offered that of the Propagation of the Faith; but each of us took a commemoration from the Mass of the other, and both recalled with a thrill of pride the marvelous things accomplished by the Apostle of the Indies in the land on which we were so soon to set foot." [37]

He was searching the dock for some missionary face.

"I said to a fellow voyager beside me: 'If you see any long-whiskered man in that line, let me know.'

"I had hardly spoken when I discovered the familiar figure of a French priest, the long black coat covering his cassock, the low, broad hat, and a wealth of beard that flowed to his cincture. With one hand shading his eyes from the sun's rays and the other holding what looked like an old-fashioned carpetbag, he was sweeping the line with penetrating glances."

Who was he?

"Every moment we were getting nearer, and now as I looked again along the wharf line, I saw the flash of a ring—

and then a photograph on file at Maryknoll came to my memory. 'The Archbishop of Tokyo!' I murmured, and—I nearly fell overboard."

At least, the European missioners were being courteous to him.

Japan was a meeting place of two ways of life: the old-fashioned native way, feudal and romantic, and the modern European materialistic way. Christian Catholic missions were not identified with either. In the sixteenth century there had been a large Catholic population in Japan, something like a million. But in the next century persecution began. Forests of crosses on which hung crucified Christians rose on the islands. Few of the million apostatized through fear. Tens of thousands were killed. "While the sun warms the earth, let no Christian be so bold as to venture into Japan," was Japan's motto.

For nigh two centuries no missioners entered Japan, yet hidden Japanese Christians continued even without priests. The heroism of these Christians was such that it was included by non-Christian Japanese in the chapter of their feudal heroism. Then, in the nineteenth century, Christian mission-ers arrived again in Japan; this time contemporaneously with Occidental materialism. They did not themselves worship at the shrine of materialism, and it was understood of them that they did not, but they were acquainted with the magic which made Europeans progressive, and which the Japanese wished to possess. Thus Christianity had also its relations with Japan's modern aspirations.

Father Walsh visited old Japan, both pagan and Christian. He went to Nikko and saw in the court of the temple "a Shinto priestess clad in white." He observed her and all things carefully: "Her face was wrinkled and solemn, and my presence made no visible impression on her. But as we stood there a small company of pilgrims stopped, and the old dame gracefully arose, opened her fan, and made some slow gyrations that drew from the respectful spectators a wealth of small coins which they threw at the feet of their priestess. . . . What impresses me, or rather depresses me, as I look into the religious customs here, is the utter absence of *love* for God." [38]

Then he went to Nagasaki, the region where the Japanese Christians had survived with such noble tenacity.

"On the run from Moji to Nagasaki, I had as companions the Belgian couple. There were also on board this train three American officers from the Philippines, and we were about the only foreign representatives until a somewhat elderly and angular American woman entered, providing entertainment for all in her vicinity.

"Her belongings occupied so much space that the Japanese man who had up to that time been enjoying life in the next seat moved to another car. Arrayed in a gray sweater and a conventional American hat, she was quick in movement and apparently a quite decided person. I could almost hear her speaking to the Sunday School children at home and to her many friends, unfolding with velocity and in well-turned, clear-cut sentences her 'wonderful' experiences in the Far East.

"She settled right down the moment the train started, laid aside her hat, pushed her suitcase under the seat, produced a roll of Japanese paper, and with her fountain pen protected by a piece of paper began the next chapter of her book— 'Japan, or Why I Was Born.' " [39]

The sight of this very American and up-to-date (speaking

in terms of 1917) young lady, who had—I suspect, although he does not say so—some disdain for him and his "Roman collar," served as a distraction from his sublime thoughts concerning the Japanese martyrs, and yet also, as a contrast, accentuated them. Even as his eye watched amusedly this lady, he became aware that he was skirting a smooth sea. It was the Bay of Omura, on the islands of which had occurred one of the most extraordinary examples of Christian perseverance in the history of the world. On those islands, Japanese Christians without priests, without altars, without any contact with Christians of other lands, without any communication with the Holy Father at Rome, and even without the knowledge that he still existed, had by their simple direct prayers to Heaven kept their faith intact during two hundred and fifty years of an existence that was more cut off from the living than the early Christian life in the catacombs, and more cut off from worldly advancement, and even more perilous.

He arrived at Nagasaki. "I had been told to look for consoling progress in the diocese of Nagasaki," he wrote, "and I knew that I should not be disappointed."

And he was not disappointed, but the voyage to Nagasaki was, in spite of the recent progress that was visible, more of a pilgrimage to the past than to the future. The story of Japanese perseverance was one of the most inspiriting ones that a missioner could hear and meditate on. In the United States it was often hard for devoted priests well supplied with altars to keep their faithful from backsliding. And why had this wonder occurred in Japan? Was it not the blood of martyrs? He thought of Théophane Vénard. He thought of the martyrs that God might some day ask of his Maryknoll.

FATHER WALSH DISCUSSES MISSION PROBLEMS WITH
MARYKNOLL SISTERS, INCLUDING TWO SISTER NURSES

But in other places, especially in Tokyo, he kept his eyes open for the developments of newer Japan, with its haste to modernize.

At Tokyo "the Academy of the Sacred Heart was a revelation. It has an extensive and excellent property on the outskirts of the city, about an hour's electric-car ride from the Cathedral. [Father Walsh, having been brought up in Boston's horsecars, still called cars not merely cars, but "electric."] It was pouring rain when we reached the convent, and as I saw the Japanese portress, and looked in on the immaculate floor, I felt like a tramp, but we went in just the same— as a tramp would have done.

"The place is already quite as extensive as some of the largest among the Sacred Heart convents in the United States, and a spacious chapel is under construction. There are twenty-three choir nuns there, and ten lay Sisters. The language school has one hundred and twenty Christians, representing many races, but most of the pupils, though not Japanese, were born in Japan. (I found Hartford, Connecticut, represented there.) The little ones, especially the Japanese Christian children, were nothing short of 'fetching' and seemed inclined, once they started, to shake a stranger's hand all day.

"We passed into the Japanese section where one hundred and eighty daughters of well-known pagan parents are taught. Here I found, besides the Sisters, Japanese lay teachers, men and women, and an opportunity was given to enter the classrooms. Catholic emblems are not wanted in this section." [40]

It had been largely due to Archbishop O'Connell of Boston, who had been sent by the Holy Father to the Emperor as

Papal Envoy in 1905, that there was now at Tokyo a Catholic College conducted by the Jesuits. Father Walsh examined this institution with special care, for it had many possibilities, and news of it had not been entirely encouraging. It scarcely competed with the Imperial University, which was a Government institution, but ten times as many students wished to enter the Imperial University as could be received; hence the Jesuits were well placed to receive those who could not be accepted by it.

"Anxious to get a better insight in the Jesuits' work, I went back as promised, for dinner, and was very kindly received.

"The main building, which is new, is constructed in red Japanese brick. The style of architecture is European—or at least not Japanese. The property covers about five acres and is of considerable value. There are eight priests under Father Hoffman, the Rector, and no fewer than seven nationalities are represented, including German, American, Swiss, French, and Japanese. Ninety students follow the courses here, and of these, some ten or twelve are Catholics.

"I left the Jesuits, convinced that they will effect much good and impressed with their condition, which, for lack of information published in the United States, I had been led to believe not altogether hopeful."

Thus he was ever correcting previous misinformation, and was making shrewd judgments. He was right in seeing a future for these Jesuits.

There was everywhere courtesy shown him in Japan by the missioners, mostly French, but not a bishop invited Maryknollers to Japan.

He next crossed the sea to Korea, which has the distinction

of being the only land in the world where the Christian Faith penetrated first simply by being carried there in a book. Some Christian books were carried to Korea from China over a century before the United States established its independence under General George Washington. They were carried there for no religious reason, but simply as part of a learned library. One reader of these books was so impressed by their teachings that he left Korea, which was utterly closed to Christians and was known, from its will to be isolated, as the Hermit Kingdom, and at Peking asked for Baptism. Then he returned to Korea and baptized some of his friends. These bookish people were so more-than-bookish that some of them were judged by Christ to be firm enough to face martyrdom. And they were martyred, and the seeds of martyrdom became four thousand converts even before a priest, in 1794, entered the land.

After that Korea was, next to Tonkin, the special land of martyrs. When Father Walsh arrived at Seoul's Cathedral, he was entering a church built above martyrs. Some of the martyrs came from "the nursery of martyrs" on the *Rue du Bac*. Henri Dorie, whose birthplace in *La Vendée* he had visited, still lay in the Cathedral, as did Father Beaulieu and Father Aumaitre. Just de Bretenières's body had rested there till 1911.

In 1910 Korea had been annexed by Japan and was governed by a Governor General. The Catholics of the country were watched over by Bishop Mutel, of Seoul, who had a majestic personality which won the respect of the Japanese and of the Koreans. "Bishop Mutel," Father Walsh wrote, "is beloved by all and presented me to various people, including the Governor General, several consuls, the Anglican Bishop, a Standard Oil man, and a couple of Protestant missionaries."

He was struck also by the happy relation which existed between Bishop Mutel and his priests. It was just such a relation as he thought appropriate to a missionary bishop. A chasm in such cases would be calamitous; equality would be wrong. It was "a slight elevation, very near, that inspires confidence"— that was the position which Bishop Mutel occupied in relation to his priests.

"I can only hope," wrote Father Walsh, "that when American missioners get to the field, their spirit will be as much as possible like that which it has been my privilege to experience in the Orient."

Bishop Mutel came nearer to inviting Maryknoll into his field than had come the bishops of Japan. He gave a hint of an invitation and might have given more, if his state of mind had not been that of a man who, pointing to the cemetery, said, "Thither is my next journey."

Father Walsh was now due to enter China. And China was to him the great field of harvest. Japan—that is, its six main islands—had but one hundred and sixty thousand square miles of area, and contained a population of fifty million. Korea had but half Japan's area, and not half her population. China had an area of two million square miles, and over three hundred million inhabitants. Moreover, she had for centuries shown herself the land for Catholic opportunity which was always being just missed. In the thirteenth century the Franciscans and Dominicans had found the Chinese ripe for conversion. Then a change of dynasty had closed China to the friars. In the sixteenth century Saint Francis Xavier, the Jesuit, had dreamed of bringing back the Faith to China as to a fabulous Cathay waiting for God's word, but he had died dramatically on her threshold, merely pointing the way. In the next century the way was taken. Highest hopes were raised of a complete conversion of the Empire. Jesuits became the Imperial wise men. Then the intellectual and spiritual crisis in Europe, rather than Chinese obduracy, wrecked those hopes. Now again the doors of opportunity had been thrown open.

The Catholic Church, though it had converted but one out of every two hundred Chinese, was well established in China. The country already had more than half a hundred vicariates or dioceses. All of them were manned—if we leave out the native priests—not by secular priests, but by members of orders or congregations or societies. The Vincentians, the Jesuits, and the Paris missioners from the *Rue du Bac* were in charge of nearly half of these vicariates, the last-named controlling six of them. Each of these vicariates had a definite relation with some European country, for the groups that tended them, even if they came from an order as international as the Jesuits, had to derive from some province in this or that European nation. There were Spanish Dominicans here, and French there. The Milan Mission Society had Hong Kong. The missioners of Shantung had been Germans of the Dutch Society of the Divine Word, and some of the Germans still stayed there, although the Japanese, in taking Shantung from the Germans, had expelled others. All these missioners, though of divers nationalities, and though representing nations which in Europe were frequently hostile one to another, were in China working together in a cause so far above others that it was mystifying to even the Chinese.

China herself was nominally at war with the German Empire, but the fighting that the Chinese were doing was largely that of faction against faction within her own borders. More than by the Yangtze River was she divided into North and South China: a demarcation line of political sentiment made the same division. In 1911 the Imperial Chinese Dynasty, that of the Manchus, had fallen, and a Republic had been instituted which found it difficult to heal North and South China into one, and to establish even a superficial order in either the North or the South. The disorders of this period of transition were a handicap to missioners: they aroused high feelings and low suspicion, they impoverished the peaceful, they made the roads unsafe. At the same time they brought to pass a misery that called for Christian charity, and that summoned Christ from heaven.

Father Walsh took the train from Seoul, up the peninsula of Korea, toward the China of great opportunity. "As our train swung to the west from Anju, I saw the sun setting over the Bay of Korea, and for a moment I thought I was taking the Maryknoll express for Ossining on a glorious November afternoon."

On Saturday morning, November 4, 1917, he woke up in Mukden, Manchuria.

Manchuria, as Father Walsh discovered from the Siberian weather which he there encountered even in November, belongs to the North, even though it is not, strictly speaking, a part of North China, being a separate region under its own name and possessed of its own special history. Mukden had a Cathedral which had been destroyed in the Boxer Uprising and was now rebuilt. At the Cathedral presided Bishop Choulet, of the Paris Foreign Missions. The Bishop was familiar to Mukden, for he had been there since 1880, and he was familiar to Father Walsh, who had often seen his photograph in the files of *The Field Afar*. At Mukden he saw other things he had known of only from books—a real mission compound surrounded by a brick wall, in which stood the Cathedral, and—which was much more trivial but which caught his eye—the compressed feet of the Chinese women.

It was only a Saturday and Sunday that Father Walsh passed at Mukden, but he saw much, for he was famished with a desire to see things Chinese, and he took many photographs— some of Chinese street scenes, others of the Mukden Cathedral seen over Mukden's roofs, others of the French Sisters who conducted an orphanage. He observed in the orphanages such orphans as he had collected cents for, while a boy of eight at the Immaculate Conception Church in Boston. He was touched by the sight of ten new arrivals, the oldest two days old, all of them laid like a single family on one of those beds of the region which had under it, for a heating system, an oven. Most of these babies had been abandoned, or had been entrusted to the Sisters lest they starve.

He gazed at them long. "The struggles of some poor human beings to keep life in their bodies make a man almost ashamed to eat a square meal. The crumbs that we American Catholics leave, and the unnecessary things that we eat, would easily feed all the abandoned babies of China." [41]

On Monday morning he took a nine-fifteen train from Mukden southward, to what was really North China, to Tientsin. All day he traveled on the way, and saw another phenomenon he had heard of as especially Chinese—floods. It was not so much the water that caught his notice, as the damage that the water had wrought, and the armies of coolies repairing the damage.

Still another Chinese phenomenon was brought to his attention—bandits. Again he did not lay eyes directly on the phenomenon; he saw no bandits. What he did see was a line-up of soldiers in every station that he passed, six of them or a dozen. It was explained to him by a Scotsman who had boarded the train at Chin-chin-fu, and who was employed by the railroad company, that these soldiers were a special police wisely selected from the families of ex-bandits to watch the first- and second-class compartments so that nothing should be stolen. "A major and captain were pointed out to me at one stop as once-notorious bandits."

At dusk he began to wonder how he would sleep. He knew that he had paid for some kind of sleeping accommodations, but just what they were he was not sure. At Chin-wang-tao he learned, for a bundle of bedding was thrown on the train, and some of it was for him. He spread a straw mat on a seat, and kept warm under it, rather than comfortable on it. At six in the morning he was at Tientsin. And there the flood was waiting for him.

He could not help being interested in this flood, since he had read so much about floods in China and seen so little of them in his own country, for Boston has no great river to drown it, and Maryknoll, although in sight of the grand Hudson, is half a mile up in the air above it. Fortunately there had been little loss of life, for the river had risen slowly. And the worst was over. He took a picture of one of the city streets which had assumed the look of Venice, for its paving was a canal. In the foreground stood one ricksha, hub-deep—which was probably his own from which he had stepped. Otherwise the canal was filled with one box serving as a boat, and a half-hundred Chinese standing deep to their waists, all of them smiling.

Tientsin was a city in process of being Occidentalized. It had eight hundred thousand inhabitants, with a considerable foreign commercial colony of five thousand persons, of whom five hundred were Americans. English was the auxiliary commercial language of the city, and a knowledge of English was valuable. This was one thing which the Catholic missioners of the place could not well give. The Bishop, a Lazarist, was a Frenchman. So were the Marists who taught a boys' school.

"Drive me to the Catholic Cathedral," he bade a ricksha man.

"Oh, the French church," the man responded, and then drove Father Walsh by mistake to the English Protestant church, thinking that, speaking English, he must be a Protestant.

But there were Catholic Americans at Tientsin, and there were some among the twelve hundred American soldiers. There was a Sister Joanna, sister of Bishop O'Connell of Richmond, Virginia, working among the French Sisters of Charity, the Superioress of whom, as soon as she heard that Father Walsh came from the land of wealth—the United States—asked him blandly for seven thousand dollars. She needed it—a flood was going on—she was in charge of a hospital.

He did find a Catholic church in which to celebrate Mass. It was that of Saint Louis. And at last he came even to the Cathedral.

"We reached the Cathedral at noon. This mission is only five years old, and I was not prepared for the surprise which I received when I saw at the end of a long street the Cathedral itself, a great pile of brick converted into a very respectable Byzantine church, large enough to hold two thousand people —at least that many Chinese. To the left was the Bishop's residence, a long two-story building enclosed by a gray brick wall. The water from the flood had been pumped over improvised dykes and the ground was muddy, but we reached the house on planks; and, as I passed along, I saw, high and dry, the scow which the priests had been using to get over to the church and down to the heart of the city." [42]

His next stop was at Peking. There he found the most famous of Catholic mission compounds—a walled-in city within a city—in the hands of the Lazarists, known as "the Peitang." He saw the Gothic Cathedral there. It was not his idea that it was best for cathedrals in China to be Gothic. But it had been designed by a French priest who thought in Gothic, and he would have blundered in any other style. He said of it: "It is the heart of the Peitang, and I was much more impressed by the original than by any photograph I had ever seen."

As a collector of money for Chinese missions and a future establisher of Maryknoll missions, he was interested in the financial problem. How had such noble buildings been erected? The answer he gave to himself in italics: *"The foresight of Catholic missioners, and their economies."* He saw evidence of the economies in the ascetic life of the Bishop who ruled the compound.

"The Bishop takes his meals with his priests in a barren-looking refectory. All rise at four A.M. Each takes his bowl of coffee and a piece of bread after Mass. Dinner and supper are served as a rule in silence; and, while the food is ample, there are no delicacies, no desserts, as Americans understand the term. Only a special vocation and the marvelous grace of God can explain the perseverance of Catholic missioners in the lives which today they are leading." [43]

It was evident everywhere that the missioners, while short-handed, having lost in the French mobilization some three hundred priests, were working very skillfully with a technique which they understood, and which they might think an outsider might not understand. He was not surprised that they did not invite the untried Maryknollers to take over a compound.

Also in Peking he met the other of the two American Sisters of Charity who were working in China. She was Sister Catherine Buschman of Baltimore. He had a talk with her. "She makes up for five."

On November 18 he arrived at the great Yangtze River, which separates North from South China. He came to it at the city of Hankow on its northern bank, which city—in so far as it was a mission—was a Franciscan city. In it he had the novel experience of parading the streets with three other American Catholic missioners—all of them Franciscans. One of them was Father Sylvester Espelage, originally of Cincinnati, who had been in China for a dozen years, and whose face had appeared, photographed, in one of the first numbers of *The Field Afar*. He had written a letter to Father Walsh, thanking him for five dollars which had become ten Chinese dollars—oh, happy days! Father Espelage now wore Chinese dress, and he seemed to speak better Chinese than the Chinese, and he received such respect everywhere that Father Walsh was amazed at him as a proof of how Chinese an American missioner could become.

After that he descended the Yangtze to the sea, and came to the city of Shanghai. On his way to Shanghai, and in Shanghai, he became familiar with another very important Chinese phenomenon, the Chinese people. He had seen them in street crowds since he entered China. He had seen their concentration and devotion at Mass. At Wuchang he visited a convent at which there were Chinese Sisters.

"I met the Chinese Sisters afterwards, and the impression which I carried away was of a very happy community of nuns, who could combine a sense of humor with serious work."

At Shanghai he encountered a very edifying individual Chinese, Lo Pa Hong, a Christian, as generous as he was rich.

"This Chinese," he wrote, "seems to be a real apostle and his one aim in life, to which everything else must be subordinated, is to save souls. He is still young—about forty-five years of age —with a large family and numerous business connections, including the direction of the Chinese Electric Car and Electric Light companies at Shanghai. He enjoys the respect of all classes of people, and his example has done immeasurable good. I am told that he serves Mass and receives Holy Communion every morning, that he makes meditation daily, recites the office of the Blessed Virgin, and says frequent rosaries, even while traveling about the city in his automobile."

It was Lo Pa Hong who had established, largely with the

aid of his friends, the great hospital of Shanghai which, though not literally a Catholic hospital, was often referred to as "Saint Joseph's." The municipality and the police supplied two thirds of the money for carrying on this institution. Mr. Lo supplied the other third with the help of his friends, among whom he included Saint Joseph as the most intimate.

Father Walsh gained a respect also for Chinese who were not Christians, and for elements in their civilization. He wished to pass on this respect to his future missioners. They must not arrive in China supercilious. Too often, in order to awaken interest in the missions, unhappy traits in Chinese civilization had been dwelt on to excess. Some Americans, for instance, had formed the conclusion that all Chinese regularly abandoned their infants. To arrive in China with such a notion would not incline the missioners to a proper respect for the Chinese. The Chinese who were confronted with such a picture of themselves would draw back with wounded sensibilities. He advised Maryknollers to respect and love the Chinese.

At Shanghai he dined with a Jesuit prelate, Bishop Paris, who was just as affable as he was uncertain whether American priests would be able "to accommodate themselves to Chinese life with its quaint customs and slow movement."

So, as Father Walsh proceeded by boat farther and farther south to Hong Kong and Canton, and was approaching Bishop de Guébriant, on whom he counted for a formal invitation to Maryknoll, he was more and more anxious lest the Bishop might have Bishop Paris's estimate of Americans rather than his own.

He encountered Bishop de Guébriant at Hong Kong. The

Bishop had not changed his mind. He offered Maryknoll a district under his jurisdiction, in his vicariate, in the Province of Kwangtung. It was called Yeungkong. Father Walsh had heard of Kwangtung, but never of Yeungkong. If Father Walsh would come to Canton, it would all be arranged.

Father Walsh did go to Canton. He met the Bishop on Christmas Day.

"When the Bishop was free, I went to his room. There, in presence of Father Fourquet, the Vicar General, and Father Souvey, who had come with me to Canton, after a prayer to the Holy Ghost, we signed the agreement by which, so far as it lay in the power of both of us, the *Catholic Foreign Mission Society of America* should be entrusted with its first mission, that of Yeungkong and Loting in the Province of Kwangtung.

"A little later the contract was on its way to Rome, and a cablegram went overseas announcing to all at Maryknoll the glad tidings that a field had been found. It was the Christ Child's gift to our young Society. May we put it to the best possible use and prove worthy of the responsibility which its possession will carry! . . .

"I had a feeling of great relief that day. It recalled an emotion experienced in Rome when, on the Feast of the Apostles Peter and Paul, June 29, 1911, in his own apartment the late saintly Cardinal Gotti gave our young Society its commission and bade it start on its task. I went to rest happy and thankful." [44]

Two weeks later came another momentous day. It was when, on January 6, 1918, from Canton he started off for Maryknoll's future mission field just as if he were Maryknoll's first missioner to it. "It was a memorable experience," he wrote, "at least for my poor self, who, during a quarter of a century, had been coddled as a priest in civilized lands."

He started off with a veteran French missioner, Father Gauthier, who would serve as his guide. They went first by boat and railroad train, and then by boat again, to Shiuhing, on the West River. So far the travel had been somewhat in European fashion. After Shiuhing it was different. The Jesuits at this unfamiliarly named city introduced him to three Chinese of his future Maryknoll field, who had been driven from it by bandits. One of them was called Ah-man; the other two, Simon Taam and A-mo Taam. These three installed him and Father Gauthier on a boat which was to take them to Maryknoll's promised land. These three launched him as missioner into missionary experiences.

The missionary experiences were not a persecution. They were simply the experiences on the Chinese boat in which he was to spend the night, laid on a shelf in a stifling, so-called stateroom, which was warmed by and forever waked by the saloon next door, in which, hidden in a cloud of joss sticks and cigarette smoke, a score of Chinese gambled long and vociferously over dominoes. In the morning he took a look at the steamer, which he had boarded at twilight and had not plainly seen. It was not a steamer at all. It had no steam. It was a gaudily painted lodginghouse that was being towed. There was at least no transatlantic vibration.

A few hours after dawn they were at Utsing, where they were taken off by a sampan, first to the wrong side of the river and then to the right side of it; that is, to Maryknoll's field.

At last Father Walsh stood a missioner in his mission. It was a region containing a million souls but with no great city. There were less than a thousand Catholics in it, and for the moment they were served by no priests. The shortage of missioners because of the World War had left it abandoned. And, more than that, it had been harried by West River pirates and by bandits.

He looked about him—Maryknoll's new fatherland for Maryknollers to love. This was South China, very far South China, and spring was in the air, and it was very hot, and he had a sore throat, yet he rejoiced in the natural beauty of the place—"the hills, the valleys rich in rice-paddies." Villages had been burned, chapels were priestless. The people were all but starving. The Christians whom they met saluted Father Gauthier, but stared at him. The place would prove a trial. He had been praying that his men might have a trial. It touched his heart, this "field afar."

After this, besides visiting the Philippines, another possible future field, he made two inevitable pilgrimages: one to the land of Tonkin, the land of martyrs and especially of Théophane Vénard, where he encountered his friend of Hawthorne, Father Cothonay; and the other to the Island of Sancian, where Saint Francis Xavier had died, waiting to enter China. It was a place where all missioners to China had a need to pray. It was China's threshold of entrance.

By the end of April, shortly after Easter, he was home in Maryknoll.

Four Maryknollers were immediately chosen to go to the China they had long dreamed of giving their lives for. They were Father Price, now fifty-seven years old, but a veteran missioner, having been acquainted with mission hardships in his twenty years in North Carolina; and Father James E. Walsh, of Cumberland, Maryland; and Father Bernard F. Meyer, of Iowa; and Father Francis X. Ford, of Brooklyn, who had run down Madison Avenue seven years before to join the Society.

There took place a departure ceremony on the eve of Our Lady's birthday, September 7, at Maryknoll. Only a few outsiders could be present, and they were not really outsiders. Father Cashin was there, and Bishop Dunn, and Father Bruneau of the Sulpicians, and Archbishop Caruana—now of Havana, then an American Army chaplain. The Seminary chapel—dedicated to Saint Paul—was a small one, and the Maryknollers themselves could fill it.

In the silence of the September evening, in the silence—the double silence—of a room in which every man present could hear his own heart, there clanged forth the smiting of a bronze bell which had come from a pagan shrine in Japan, and had been presented to Father Walsh on his tour of the East. At the voice of it, as at a summons from the far Orient, there emerged from the chapel's sacristy, out before the altar, the four missioners—Maryknoll's first, their long training at an end, their battle begun.

They were but entering Maryknoll's own sanctuary; but they were starting for the field which he, their commander, had opened for them, and which he, with his calm, prescient eyesight, had explored.

The Builder

THE DECADE and more, that began in 1918 and ended in September, 1929, brought to many things in the United States a very rank growth, some of it healthy-stalked, some of it rotten, but all of it extraordinarily visible to the eye. The Empire State Building in New York City grew so high that it could be seen from Sunset Hill thirty-four miles away.

During this decade Maryknoll was one of the things that grew. From a veranda-ed boardinghouse above the Hudson, looking like a hundred others, it grew into a noble building of field stone, with a green-tiled roof and with Oriental curves to the roof, which had no counterpart, and which tourists strained their necks looking at as they sped by in automobiles. Its pagoda-ed tower nodded to the Empire State Building. But it was the Empire State Building that was amazed.

Maryknoll's mission force, its expeditionary corps, grew from an army of four which went ridiculously in the wrong direction, while Pershing's army was being ferried to France in millions, to an army of eighty, which, after Pershing's army had been disbanded, was in China winning honors. It was in Kongmoon that the army of four had begun its campaign, and there that it had gained its first spiritual victories.

In 1924 Kongmoon had been erected by Propaganda into a prefecture apostolic, all of it under the charge of Maryknoll. It was no small responsibility, for it was in area as large as Ohio, and it had about the same population. In it in the same year was included the Island of Sancian, on which Saint Francis Xavier had died trying to enter China—wherefore the island had become the most precious Christian relic in China. The very possession of it conferred on its possessor an honor like that of the possession of the highest military decoration.

And then in 1927 the chief of this Kongmoon expeditionary force, who was Father James Edward Walsh, had been raised to be Bishop.

Everything about Maryknoll grew. The number of subscribers to *The Field Afar* grew from forty thousand in 1918 to one hundred and twenty thousand in 1929. The secretaries, or "Teresians" as they were later called, grew into the Foreign Mission Sisters of Saint Dominic, three hundred strong, of whom one half were at Sunset Hill and a third in the Orient. Miss Mary Rogers became their first Mother General. The Auxiliaries of Saint Michael grew to a lay Brotherhood fifty in number. The mission field of Maryknoll grew until it included a vicariate and a prefecture in South China. Maryknoll also had missions in Manchuria, in Korea, in the Philippines, and in Hawaii. Then there were the home missions which had sprung up at Seattle, at Los Angeles, and at San Juan Bautista in California. The schools of Maryknoll had multiplied. There was a new preparatory seminary—like The Vénard—on the heights of Los Altos, overlooking the Santa Clara Valley near San Francisco. There was a House of Studies in Washington, D. C., at the Catholic University.

There was a *Collegio Maryknoll* in Rome. Maryknoll's buildings were sprouting like spring asparagus on a sunny day. They came up behind you as you moved.

Of all this growth, Father Walsh had been the animator. He had possessed the courage for expansion, which had shocked his "business" friends, who even in these times of "business" optimism had interjected: "But where will you get the money?"

To which he would reply, mocking them gently, "It's God's affair."

He was the Society's Superior, and Treasurer, and Rector of its Seminary at Ossining. He was the editor of its *Field Afar*. He could not even count on help from his cofounder, Father Price, for the latter was in China.

In December, 1918, Father Price had arrived at Yeungkong, and from the mission church of Our Lady of Lourdes had written on December 21:

"Here we are at last, all of us—safe and sound and happy. We arrived at eleven o'clock last night, all worn out; came in a sailing boat the last twenty-five miles, as the captain of the Chinese junk refused to budge from where he was for another twenty-four hours or so. We thought of cabling our arrival but found it would cost fifteen dollars, and so I am writing this at the first moment. The whole place is much better than we thought. A few Christians had festooned the front of the church to greet us, came to Mass, shot off firecrackers in our honor, paid us a visit, and insisted on giving us a special dinner. I will write more at length in a few days, when I get settled.

"Father Gauthier is with us, engineering all things. We left

Bishop de Guébriant in Canton on Wednesday night after receiving his blessing and good wishes." [45]

But in the following September Father Price died of an acute attack of appendicitis, at Saint Paul's Hospital, Hong Kong. His body stayed for sixteen more years in China, until, after the death of Father Walsh, it was brought to Maryknoll; but his heart, by his own bequest, was sent to Nevers in France to be near the body of Saint Bernadette.

Father John I. Lane had never been in any sense a third founder of Maryknoll. All too conscious of his ill health, he had merely asked for, and received, a temporary release from the Boston Archdiocese in order to make a try of the Maryknoll life, which in the end had proved too much for him. Yet he had been a contemporary of Father Walsh's, who knew what Father Walsh was seeking for, and who knew all about the beginnings of Maryknoll, and from him Father Walsh could have received counsel concerning Maryknoll's future. But he, too, had died.

Father Stanton had died.

There were distinguished members of the American hierarchy who gave Father Walsh every encouragement. But they could shoulder no responsibilities. Should he make a blunder, the blunder would be his, not theirs.

He had young Maryknollers of enterprise, who were heads of his missions in China. They had learned to take the responsibilities that they had to take. They had shown initiative not only in the Orient but even at home. One of these missioners— Bishop James E. Walsh, of Kongmoon—had not only directed the building of his own residence and pro-cathedral in China, but in the United States had collected the money for the same—all of it, forty thousand dollars, in the Boston Archdiocese. But these heads of his missions, while they could govern for him afar, could not govern with him at home.

From other young Maryknollers who were more accessible, he could ask for advice. From an advisory Council of four, he could demand advice. But they were of a different generation. They looked to him as to a leader. And he had to act as their leader.

Father Walsh, and he alone, was the animator of Maryknoll; he, and he alone, was the promoter of its growth. And he, and he alone, was the orderer of its growth so that its growth should be sane.

Solitary, from an eminence, which Providence had given to him rather than which he had chosen, he surveyed his growing Maryknoll in its entirety. Others were busy with details; he had to coordinate details. He had to watch and safeguard both the material and the spiritual aspect, and everywhere. He fed here and pruned there like a busy gardener, and like a gardener who knows the extent and design of his garden, and who does not sacrifice the whole for one of its parts. China was a part of his garden difficult to look at. He contrived, none the less, to keep acquainted with the Chinese situation. He had his own experience in China to look back on. And he could read not only the lines, but what lay between the lines, of the letters of his missioners. And he could revisit China. Twice in a decade he revisited it: once with his friend, Father James F. Kelly of the Boston Archdiocese; and then in 1926 with another priest friend, Father John J. Crane. His Maryknoll had a sensitive relation to Rome. Of that, too, he kept track. He was a pilgrim to Rome in 1926 with Father Crane, on their

A FAREWELL TO MARYKNOLL MISSIONERS ASHORE AS
THE RIVER JUNK DEPARTS

way to the East. Every year he visited the Maryknoll establishments in the United States.

As the Superior of Maryknoll, he had to assume the responsibility which every superior anywhere must exercise, the right use of which is necessary to his office. He delegated authority. There will never be, in spite of all the intelligence and character tests which psychologists may elaborate, any sure mechanical method for a superior to pick his assistants. Some superiors pretend to take a long time in making the choice, and others of them do. Generally they decide by intuition quickly, by regarding a face, and then they try to explain their choice logically thereafter. Father Walsh did not conceal the fact that he believed he could see much in a face. Neither did he conceal from himself that he had at times been deceived by a face. But however that may be, he did choose his subordinates with a discernment that warranted his being Superior. Saint Francis of Assisi, Saint Ignatius Loyola, all founders of religious orders, incurred vicissitudes through mistakes they made in delegating authority, and yet they were admirable superiors. Father Walsh encountered fewer vicissitudes than they. He must have done fairly well in choosing his lieutenants.

He was also, on his lone eminence, Maryknoll's Treasurer. This was a task which required not only fortitude but technical financial skill. He had to economize, and to watch details of expense.—Put out the lights. It's only one light, and counts little. No, it counts.—But parsimony is common enough. He had also to collect money, and to use it well, even on projects which to some seemed extravagant. He had to make proper contracts, and borrow money, if at all, wisely.

It is true that he had an enormous trust in God. *Deus providebit.* But God had made him Treasurer, and a treasurer could be no obscurantist. He had to have both eyes open, and even to have eyes in the back of his head. Eternal vigilance was the price of solvency. He always knew where he stood, what his debts were, and what his assets, and what was the relation of his financial predicament to the financial condition of the whole country, and of the whole world.

It was his custom to send out circular letters to Mary-knollers far and wide, at least twice a year, and in these he gave occasionally summaries of Maryknoll's financial situation, which were models of lucidity, never over-anxious, never falsely jubilant. In 1921 he wrote:

"Our financial condition is relatively good, although you might not think so if I told you that we were saddled with a debt of two hundred thousand dollars and are facing a building proposition of a half million. We have against this, however, the clientele of *The Field Afar,* and while proportionately our appeals today do not produce the result of earlier days, perhaps because of multiplied missionary activities, we are buoyed up by the feeling that we have in our paper a strong right arm. At the present time, however, we are hardly in a position to advance money to other sections of our work, and we must depend upon the activities of these sections to bring about the desired means of subsistence. Fortunately, all our branches and the missions themselves have in *The Field Afar* a 'big brother' who can and will gladly talk for them, but they must in turn stimulate the 'big brother,' whose attention is constantly engrossed by a multitude at home dragging on his coat tails."

The next year he had another financial comment to make:

"The debts are occasioned largely by building operations at the Center and by subsidies (technically loans) to The Vénard. We could hardly have had higher costs of labor and material, but we had to accept the figures as we were practically forced to build.

"The per capita cost has been reduced, however, and leaks are better watched as the years go on. If within the next ten years we can complete the Seminary and The Vénard, and provide a building quite as large to be occupied by our Sisters, we shall be most fortunate." [46]

It was not only The Vénard and the major Seminary that he had to keep track of financially.

There was China!

"From China comes a call for $200,000, with the assurance that a million dollars would hardly cover the needs suggested by openings across the Pacific, with works in Hong Kong, possibilities in Canton—and crying needs in all the missions." [47]

There was Seattle!

"Seattle is struggling without a resident priest, but the Sisters and Brother Martin are keeping up a growing work for Japanese. A club of Catholic laymen failed to realize their expectations, and the house at Seattle with a debt of $10,000 must be mothered, and is looking to Maryknoll in the event of special need." [48]

Intimately connected with money was *The Field Afar,* for by it and through it came his best resources. The magazine was his great expression of confidence in the American public. It was his earthly petition to earthly men in God's name, and he wished to have it do its petitioning well; not too assertively, but frankly and confidently. To have his petitioning eloquent, he had need of the collaboration of his missioners, and he advised them on the nature of the letters and the photographs that he expected from them.

"In the midst of your numerous occupations and at times difficult surroundings, your letters have come frequently. All of them have been welcome, and we have been in a position to make use of much that you have sent. Photographs have been not overplentiful, but we have managed to get something that would reproduce and interest.

"Your narratives are unstilted and evidently true to facts without exaggeration. I hope that this example which the 'ancients' have set will be strictly followed by all. *No exaggeration* should be a watchword, whether the letter be written to Maryknoll or to a private correspondent. Any of your letters, however private, may yet appear in print, and one false statement can do harm to the cause.

"Don't fear to strike the humorous note occasionally. It is a humorous note that attracts readers to more serious portions of your letter. Keep in mind, too, that we are hungry for quaint sayings, odd customs and 'breaks,' as also for photographs of your daily life, especially such photos as show life in unconscious repose. We need also material for stories, if not the stories themselves." [49]

Another of Father Walsh's activities was the supervision of the design and construction of Maryknoll's buildings. Those of his missioners in China were beyond his ken. If he gave any instruction at all in regard to them, it was the general instruction of Rome, that where possible the native tradition should be respected. He left their designing to his missioners. But at home, in the United States, he gave more than hints to the architects. He took a hand, when the buildings were near enough to him, even in their interior decoration. This was not that he prided himself on a rare architectural sense, which indeed he possessed. Nor was it any kind of officiousness. There are sermons in stones, and he wished them to say the right thing. Maryknoll's buildings should look like buildings that belonged to Maryknoll. Their interior walls should be hung with decorations which taught not only a love of God, but a respect for the peoples whom God had made, to whom the Maryknollers were going as missioners. Let Oriental prints that witnessed to the artistic ability of the Chinese, and also portrayed their civilization, be displayed in this corridor and that refectory. At The Vénard he was discovered hanging the proper pictures in the proper places with his own hands.

Maryknoll's mission of San Juan Bautista in California was, of course, not of his designing, nor had he watched its building. It was now being used by his Maryknoll priests to care for Americans, Mexicans, and Japanese; but it had once been used by the Spanish Franciscans for the "Digger" Indians of the Pacific Coast. It had been built by the Franciscans in the eighteenth century, and its beauty was theirs. Yet its beauty was by him appreciated, and through him was woven into the scheme of Maryknoll buildings.

At Los Altos, near San Francisco, a junior seminary of Maryknoll was erected according to his wishes, in a mission style that related it to San Juan Bautista, and related the work of his foreign missioners to that of the Spanish foreign missioners who had prepared his path.

The building most his was the central Seminary on Sunset Hill. The Boston architectural firm of Maginnis and Walsh—of which his brother Timothy was the Walsh—did its designing, but he was at their elbow. He wanted this or that practical detail, for his Seminary was not merely to be photographed: it had to be lived in. It must fit the needs of a seminary, and the activities of a seminary. A recreation room would have to be not where it looked best, but where it served best. And the building had to be so designed that it could be self-sufficient even before it was entirely completed. And it must not cost too much. At the same time it had, in its outward appearance, to symbolize Maryknoll's purpose. It was his prompting, as well as the ingenuity of Maginnis and Walsh, that had it assume its Oriental aspect of curved Chinese roof and pagoda-like tower in which showed the Oriental beams of lacquer-red and lacquer-green. It was to suit him that the architects at the same time gave it its Occidental solidity, and its native American touch of being walled out of Westchester County field stones dragged from the fields and ravines of Maryknoll's own farm. Thus it grew permanent as Rome, yet winged with an Oriental lightness as if ready to fly to the East and there be at home next to the palaces Marco Polo had wondered at in Hangchow, "the City of Heaven."

The very site of it was his choosing and his gaining. The land on which it was to be built did not originally belong to Maryknoll's ninety acres. Its owner held out for a price exorbitant. Accordingly he staked out his Seminary on some of his own land. Surreptitiously at the same time, the Maryknoll Sisters buried a medal of Saint Joseph on the desired land.

Together he and his Sisters won the day. The owner woke up one morning suddenly reasonable. The land was bought.

Begun in 1919, the Seminary found its foundations soon entirely dug, and the plan was envisaged of completing the structure within five years. But he noted that numerous other American missionary establishments were enlisting recruits. And he was glad of it. They, too, were building houses. "Go slowly," he counseled himself. By 1929 the building was not half finished. The discreet retardation of construction was also his.

More important than anything else was the spiritual stewardship of his flock. In this expansion their egotism must not be expanded, nor must their spirit grow lax. In his Christmas letter to Maryknollers, in 1927, he wrote:

"God's blessing has been so visible in our work at home and abroad, even in trials, that we may be confident it will never fail us. The measure of His bounty is limitless, we know, and it will fill our every need in proportion as we keep ourselves down and our souls open.

"Pray that I may be mindful of this condition in the year that faces us, and be assured of my prayers for you."

He wanted them as a Society to be humble and to rely on God, yet each individual of them had to be hardened to his work:

"No one of us stands alone. We are interdependent, and the success of Maryknoll missions is measured by the perfection of each individual member. We are thought to be generous— more so even than the average priest in the homeland—and it can be presumed that no Maryknoller entered on what he considered his lifework who was not actuated by a fine spirit of generosity.

"But—with the passing of time, the soul of a priest experiences change, for better or for worse; and generous hearts, even those of missioners, can contract.

"To be safe, we must cultivate detachment, because it is the sure way to real love for God. If we grow attached to anything created, to our own comfort, to time-wasting and useless recreation, to natural occupations, to food, to drink, to money, or to social pleasures, we shall find ourselves drawing away from God and His consolations.

"The grace of God is surely at our hand in abundant measure because thousands are praying and making sacrifices for us. May we each and all—above all, myself—prove praiseworthy." [50]

They should be praiseworthy, yet not praising themselves, not even looking at their own selves. They must not think that they were the only apostles in the world, or that their foreign-mission activity was the only thing going on in this world. Nor must any Maryknoller think of himself as more important than another. Nor must any Maryknoller dream in luxurious, spiritual self-indulgence, "Without me, nothing can go on."

He taught a spirit of selflessness partly by necessary sermonizing reiteration, but mostly by his own Catholic spirit. Speaking of his own dear plan to complete his symbolic and majestic Seminary, he had written:

"Personally, I might never see the completion of our Seminary. It matters little, and perhaps for my soul's sake it will be better so. All that we can do is give our best effort, and wait for God's time.

"Let us pray for each other. We do so now, but we can do better."

This was written in 1923. Four years later he wrote in the same tone:

"My prayer for you is the prayer that I will ask of you for myself, that during 1927 I may strive to know myself better, more as God knows me; that I may note the failings in myself and what is best in others; that, as a consequence, I may think less about myself and more about God and others, keeping close to all with whom I am associated in His glorious work."

Father Walsh treated the other missionary societies recruiting in the United States not as rivals, but as cooperators. "To those who love God, all things work together for good." It would indeed be unfortunate if, because his Society had the inclusive name of Catholic Foreign Mission Society of America, it should think it was a monopoly. He worked with the Fathers of the Society of the Divine Word in promoting the Catholic Students' Mission Crusade. When the Irish Maynooth Mission of Saint Columban wished to establish an American branch, he acted as host to those who wished to do the establishing, and had the Reverend Doctor Blowick address his students. It was not of Maryknoll's vocation only that he was thinking, but of the country's.

President Wilson in 1918 had said: "It is not an army that we must shape and train for war: it is a nation." Father Walsh was not merely training Maryknoll: he was training the United States.

And what could alienate him more from the nation than the assuming of a proud attitude that only foreign missioners counted? He took an interest in all the religious developments in his country, encouraging movements that had no direct relation to China, such as the liturgical revival and the street-corner speaking of Mrs. Martha Moore Avery and Mr. David Goldstein. When *The Commonweal*—a Catholic weekly—was in danger of dying through poverty, he mentioned its predicament in his *Field Afar*. He was one of the Patrons of the Saint Paul's Guild for converts, and a firm friend of the magazine, *Liturgical Arts*. He sent some of his students to the Pius X School of Liturgical Music. He kept his hand on the pulse of the country.

And especially he kept his hand on the pulse of his friends. A superior of a foreign-mission seminary should not dehumanize himself, nor separate his specialized charity. His very particular boon companion, Father Stanton, had died in 1922, but he had other friends in the Boston priesthood. Then there were his relatives: his brother Timothy; and his cousin, Mrs. Patrick Tracy (daughter of the Mrs. Daniel Shea to whom he was so indebted); and his sister, Mrs. Thomas B. Hughes, and her children. To the Hughes family he wrote always at least twice a week, usually shortly, but in his own handwriting.

Once when there was sickness in the family, he wrote:

"It must pain you keenly to be conscious of any physical weakness, especially when accompanied by suffering in your own child. I believe, however, that the ills of children have their purpose in forming character, and that a pain-free, sturdy growth, full of health, is not always a blessing, whatever the world has to say about it. What beautiful souls we often meet in weak bodies! And how easily pride and selfishness find entrance where physical perfection and unstinted abundance are constant!" [51]

In the spring of 1924, Mrs. Hughes's son, Jack, was confirmed. Father Walsh almost forgot it, but not quite.

"A trip to Washington threw me off on my reckoning, and your Confirmation day passed without a line from me. I wish you to know, however, that I am thinking of you, and pray that God the Holy Ghost may keep you always strong in the blessed Faith of your childhood.

"You will find life a battle, but God's grace is always ready for us and will enable us to conquer every difficulty.

"I hope you, too, have the name 'Joseph.' Saint Joseph was humble and loved Jesus. He is now the Patron of the Universal Church, the silent but much-loved saint."

And two weeks later he was writing him again:

"I am pleased to know that you have the name 'Joseph.'

"I see that you are about to be graduated from the grammar school and will go from there to the Cambridge Latin. It is a step in your life that will bring you into a different atmosphere, and you will not have the same spiritual helps that you have had up to the present time. But I feel that your foundation is good and strong, so that there will be no fear for you.

"Keep up your frequent Communions, and be ready always to serve others whenever it is in your power to do so. This will strengthen you spiritually and will bring its own reward. There is no happiness better in this life than that which we experience in trying to make others happy."

With another group of friends he kept in close contact, the

families of his Maryknollers. He knew well enough from looking in his own heart, as well as by hearing the occasional ex-
postulations that came from them, that they were making
great sacrifices in sending their kin into exile. Generally they
were religious families—otherwise the mission vocations would
not have come from their midst—yet few of them had envisaged the sacrifice which God asked of them. He insisted
on treating them as special friends and as collaborators. In
their case it was not so much letters that he wrote to them,
as visits that he made. Whenever his tours of inspection took
him about the country, he called at their front doors, and entered in the American "homes of martyrs."

He was also Rector of Maryknoll's Center, and had the
spiritual responsibility for all the students of rapidly growing
Maryknoll. They must not be too uplifted individually, nor
overproud of their Maryknoll in general.

To keep his Maryknollers from individual self-importance,
it was not his idea to treat them with Draconian severity. He
chose rather to keep in them a family spirit. This had been
easy enough when the family was a small family. Then his
emphasis had been rather on giving them an idea that familiarity is a noble thing, not a spirit of informal camping-out together. Let nothing, even when Maryknoll was a leaky cottage
without a decent pump, be done as if in makeshift.

"I have loved poverty ever, dirt never," he quoted from Saint
Bernard. He insisted on order and decorum.

Within this decorum a seemly family spirit could take care
of itself. Just how far the familiarity could be carried is illus-
trated by the recorded letter of one of his first students, who
happened to be the future Father Francis X. Ford:

THE SEMINARIANS GREET THE SUPERIOR GENERAL AS HE RETURNS FROM THE FAR EAST

". . . I do not like to annoy you, but would you ask someone to let my turtle free? I left him near the pump and had
no time to attend to him. Perhaps Father McCabe might like
to train him; a turtle is much more interesting than a canary."

Such a spirit of familiarity was so good a thing that it had
to be guarded from abuse. One day, several years later, when
Maryknoll was still small, Father Walsh heard one of his
students calling up someone in New York on the telephone,
telling the someone that Father Walsh would be passing
through the city and would pick up his valise. This was news
to Father Walsh, and he had sense enough to be angry. When
the student turned round from the telephone, he found himself face to face with his Superior, who for the instant towered to the sky. Yet that evening, when Father Walsh returned from New York, the valise was in his hand.

When Maryknoll grew, when its new Seminary at Sunset
Hill was containing a hundred students, when it had colleges
on the Pacific Coast and in Pennsylvania, Father Walsh wished
to keep what was best in this family spirit, but let it not be
thought that he maintained it by an indiscriminate and
forced familiarity. He was a very personal man. When he met
you, when he was first introduced to you, his handshake was
firm, and his gaze was steadfast upon you. He had a lip sensitive as if ready to speak, but it said almost nothing. He was not
interested in making an impression; he was interested in you.
You who were being looked at had a feeling that he might
or might not like you, but that he was really concerned with
you, and that if a cannon went off behind him he would not
turn his head. There was something precious in you. His
arched eyebrows seemed to give him a perspective deep into

you. You were you. Such a man was not made for indiscriminate familiarity.

His wit was for the few—except when he wrote as a journalist—or it was for a crowd on rare occasions. A play is a play, and he encouraged plays and the writing of plays among his students, and when he attended them he was not so much "the Superior" as a partaker in the mirth. He would explain in attending that he came principally to see if he could find some of the lost furniture of Maryknoll or his own lost raiment being used as stage properties.

When it was his office to be jocund, he could play the master at it. At The Vénard during vacation months, it was the custom to open the property to outside youths for a summer camp. There was a faculty table on a dais, where the faculty ate, he with them if he was at The Vénard. The older boys at this camp wished one day to play on a newcomer one of the tricks that veterans like to play on tyros. The veterans told a newcomer that it was the custom for newcomers to eat their first meal at the high table where Father Walsh happened to be. Up marched the innocent to his fancied discomforting. Father Walsh was not going to be outmatched by schoolboys. The boy in him recognized what had happened, and with perfect gravity he played his part, entertaining the guileless, foolish newcomer as a wise visiting prince.

When the dictum was going round this country that "Poverty will be abolished," he kept his students sane, and was not afraid in so doing to get rid of those who would better not have entered. The world had not changed. A vocation for foreign missions was not for everyone; it required heroism. Nothing was more unfair to a student than to keep him as a future Maryknoller simply by easy kindness of heart, when an apparent cruelty would be to the young man a saving of his future. He never tried to deceive the enthusiasts into thinking that a crest of the wave was a good thing to ride on.

All this directing—financial, material, and spiritual—took time. And the wonder of these years, when Father Walsh had to do so much alone, was that he did not break down under the strain. That he could keep his head high was largely due to the same thrift of time that he had shown in Union Park Street. He did one thing at a time. One task almost rested him from another. This thrift of time is difficult to describe: it took place so much within his own brain. Yet it had visible manifestations, which, though minor and even trivial, yet illustrate it. Take one of them. No one takes up so much time as a visitor. Hospitality merely encourages the visitor to prolong his pleasant interview, beyond its importance. Yet hospitality is necessary. Father Walsh had two watches: a wrist watch from which to tell the time, and a large family watch which could be used to dismiss visitors from before his desk, with celerity and yet no apparent discourtesy. It was such a handsome, ceremonious, polite watch! He would take it from his pocket with gracious, attentive gesture, and the visitor would leave without knowing why he left.

By the year 1929 Maryknoll had, by its growth, attracted an extraordinarily wide notice in the United States. Missionary societies in general attract little attention in the loud news of the day, but this missionary Society became "news." Quite aside from its spirit, it caught the eye by its apparent material success. In "journalese" language it was the great Catholic achievement of the century. It was also a sample of American energy. In Rome, which has seen many a rapid growth come to no fruition, it attracted attention for different reasons: it was healthy; it was humble.

As early as 1921 Father Walsh had received congratulations from Rome. Pope Benedict XV had written to him:

"Beloved Son, health and apostolic benediction.

"More than once have We praised the zeal which has long been active in America for the progress of the missions among the heathen; and at the same time We have rejoiced in the abundance of choice fruit obtained with God's help by the Catholic Foreign Mission Society of America, over which you preside. But now We wish again heartily to congratulate you, since recently We have learned from several sources, and especially from the Archbishop of New York, that this work is flourishing more and more. This indeed, after God, must be attributed to the ability of yourself and your associates; for, burning with zeal for souls, you leave nothing undone that the light of the Gospel with a more civilized life may enlighten the nations that still sit in darkness."

His successor, Pope Pius XI, known as the Pope of Missions, had continued to look hopefully yet critically at a mission from which so much might come, should it be successful. He was pleased with the vivacity of the Americans, and still more pleased with the vivacity when it showed that it was accompanied with perseverance. He even read regularly the vivacity of *The Field Afar*. When in 1925 he inaugurated a Mission Exposition in his Vatican Gardens, he glanced with special expectation at Maryknoll's own individual exhibit, which was arranged by Father Considine of Maryknoll. Father Considine later attracted his attention by initiating the *Fides News Service,* which acquainted Catholics with what went on in the farthest reaches of the world and kept them with the fullness of the globe of the world before their eyes. The Holy Father was pleased with Maryknoll, not because of its size, but because it had a sense of the size of the world.

In 1928 Father Walsh crossed the Atlantic for a special visit to Rome. He had special business there, Maryknoll business. Father Winslow of Maryknoll was already at Rome before him; Father Ford of Kaying, China, went from Asia over the Indian Ocean to meet him. Maryknoll had grown so much that it ought in size to be considered as of age. Its growth, moreover, had been so happily trimmed that it had a shape; it could be considered as of the age of reason. In other words, Maryknoll was ready to adopt permanent Constitutions, just as if it were to continue like the perennial orders and congregations of the Church—Benedictines, Sulpicians, Jesuits, Vincentians.

There took place in Rome various meetings which are of interest to students of canon law and to ecclesiastics. Rules and regulations were considered with Roman thoroughness. Father Nolan of the Dominicans was consulted. Father Ford was consulted: how was this rule to be phrased to meet Chinese conditions? Finally a complete draft of proposed Constitutions was left with Archbishop Marchetti-Selvagiani, the Secretary of Propaganda, who made his corrections. It was then to be brought home to America for further discussion by the Society, and adoption by it. Then it would go back to Rome for final approval.

But, before leaving Rome, the Maryknoll party and the Maryknoll students at Rome were received in audience by the Pope of the Missions. It was December 4. To Father Walsh the Holy Father said:

"We are acquainted with your Society, and with what it is doing. It has expanded well, and wherever it is, it is working hard. For your Society, then, all the blessings that you desire! We are following it with great interest and with joy."

Then he went on, turning to the Maryknoll students from the *Collegio Maryknoll,* who also were present:

"And for your students a very special blessing, because, when we speak of novices and of students, we are speaking of the future. Really they are the future. We say *few* and *good;* not quantity but quality, *n'est-ce-pas?*"

Once again he turned to Father Walsh, and in lower voice:

"And then we also say *good* and *many.* For you, may it be thus!" [52]

In the following August—August, 1929—a chapter of the Society was held, with delegates at it from China, Manchuria, and Korea, and from the other Maryknolls then established. There were sixteen delegates present, comprising all ordinaries and superiors of the Society, representatives of missions, and the members of the Council, besides elected delegates. It was no mere "business" or merely legal affair. It was a solemn coming of age. Before each session a passage from the Acts of the Apostles was read. The Superior made a preliminary address:

"We have registered failures and successes, but so far we seem to have won the regard of the Catholic body in our own country, the substantial good will of our European confreres, and, best of all, the confidence of our superiors at Rome; and this in spite of human weakness manifest in ourselves individually and in the body to which we belong."

There followed no careless optimism and precipitate adoption. Maryknoll was of age: it had acquired its wisdom under Father Walsh's directions. It should use that wisdom. Each clause of the Constitutions was considered separately and voted on separately. Then Maryknoll did its adoption of it.

Forthwith reports were read in detail by the Superior at home and those of his subordinates who were in charge of missions abroad. There was no boasting, no self-complacence. Whatever the public might think, they of Maryknoll were aware that the brief show of success had not put an end to dangers ahead. They were thinking of the future—the fickle future. And the present is ever attended with dangers.

After a week of meetings, the elections were held. Father Walsh was chosen Superior General, but he could now cease to be Rector and Treasurer. He would have a regular Council of four Assistants who would help him with his decisions. They were elected, and were: Monsignor Patrick J. Byrne, of Pengyang in Korea; Father Raymond A. Lane, of Fushun, Manchuria; Father James M. Drought, who had been working in Manila; and Father William F. O'Shea.

Maryknoll, launched in weather somewhat fair, yet speeding on its voyage through weather wondrous fair, was ready to continue its voyage, come what might.

The Strengthener

FOOLS FLOURISH. There's something rotten. The storms come.

"Havoc!" cried the ticker tape in October, 1929, and down to the ground tumbled a fictitious prosperity.

Men who had staked their all on a dream of perpetual prosperity went about with pipe-clay faces, moribund. The prophets of a fantastic hope tried to keep their troops from panic, going among them bravely, calmly: "Prosperity is just around the corner."

Father Walsh was not moribund with panic, nor did he protest that nothing had happened—it had.

During his sixty-two years of life, he had encountered half-a-dozen business depressions. They had even come periodically since the Declaration of Independence. But they had all been passed over, owing to the fact that this country, although somewhat a business venture, was a lot more. Men had had their religious convictions and religious hopes, which were fanatical sometimes, erroneous very often—but which none the less attached men to an eternal destiny and steadied them. This was the first depression which the United States experienced in which its hopes were mainly placed on a perpetual financial prosperity. And when that hope was shaken, everything was being shaken. He knew it. Maryknoll might be shaken.

A mere financial panic would have been a serious inconvenience to Maryknoll in 1929, though not a disaster. Maryknoll had a hundred missioners to support in the Far East, and it had mortgages to pay off. It required a very large income, which had to be collected from the spare dollars of friends of Maryknoll. But those friends were not the people who would be most affected by the gyrations of the stock market. Very few of them were active financiers, and not many of them were even well-to-do. It was the comparatively unmoneyed who gave most; and, though they might be somewhat poorer, and might be forced to give somewhat less, their poverty was used to being generous.

But this was more than a merely financial panic; it was moral, and the danger to Maryknoll lay in the possibility that the public might turn its back on Maryknoll as it was turning its back on almost all the wonder-things it had for a decade cherished and boasted of. There was scarcely a leader who had been adulated in early 1929 who, in early 1930, was not being repudiated with fierce spleen. The chief scapegoats were businessmen who, some of them, deserved the disfavor they received. But statesmen, good and bad, suffered also. And why might not the Catholic public turn upon Father Walsh? "You brought us to this wastefulness and folly!" And then turn from him.

It was on the twenty-fourth of October that the financial crash began on the New York Stock Exchange. On the morning of October 30, the financial public—and all of the United States, including newsboys, was the financial public—was aghast to read in the newspapers that on the preceding day over sixteen million shares had been poured into the market to be sold, and they were still more aghast to find that the value of shares was disappearing like a piece of newspaper held in a flame. They were aghast, a large number of them, no doubt because their earthly fortune was shrinking, but more, they were aghast because they were bewildered and the human mind does not like to be bewildered. Even a success which comes with bewilderment is not wholly welcome, and is forgotten in consternation. There are nights, for instance, when we have asked that dawn delay, so that we can recover from fatigue; but if the sun should really be an hour late, we should be more upset by the unexpectedness than pleased by the boon granted. There were a few who gained money by the crash in the stock market, but there was scarcely a one who was contented in his success. Even those who had won in financial speculation were unsteadied by the general unsteadiness. They were as if blindfolded and fearsome. Weeks and months went by, and soon even the masters of finance—the most candid of them—began to acknowledge that they as well as all others were in the dark.

And in the dark a prominent industrialist, Charles M. Schwab, said or is reported to have said: "I'm afraid; every man is afraid. I don't know, we don't know, whether the values we have are going to be real next month or not." [53]

Father Walsh was not a worshiper of Dagon or Plutus or any other god of earthly prosperity, and he knew perfectly

well what values would last in the long run. He was not himself perturbed. He was not even perturbed lest the Maryknollers should be perturbed. In August, 1930, he wrote to his
Maryknollers a letter which was called forth by the approval
which Rome had recently given to Maryknoll's Constitutions.

"May each of us accept these *Constitutions,* their interpretation, and any insistence on their observance, as God's will in
our regard, and as a blessed means to a strong union of hearts,
minds and wills. All for Christ!

". . . I wish here and now to include my own act of thanksgiving and acknowledgment to you and to all Maryknollers,
who have made possible this spiritual development of our Society during this period of test—and have succeeded in drawing from our superiors this supreme manifestation of their
confidence and good-will." [54]

This voice in August, 1930, had the same ring in it that it
had had in 1929.

As for the Catholic public who had been supporting him
with prayers and alms, he would give them courage, by showing courage, and by treating them as if they, as he liked to
think, possessed it. He went ahead with the expansion of
Maryknoll.

He and his four Assistants did arrange for certain economies. They sold their House of Studies at the Catholic University. But where growth was necessary to the carrying out of
God's work, there they did not prune: they encouraged
growth.

Among the archbishops who had especially favored Maryknoll—a list which included Cardinal Farley; and Arch-

bishop Hanna, of San Francisco; and Archbishop Dowling, of Saint Paul; and, perhaps the initially most important, Cardinal O'Connell of Boston—there was Archbishop McNicholas, of Cincinnati. He was, to begin with, a Dominican, and the Dominicans had had some special relations with Maryknoll. The Dominicans of Hawthorne had since 1913 provided the Maryknoll Seminary with a theological faculty, which now consisted of the white-robed, year-in-and-year-out Fathers McHugh and Callan, outstanding scholars who had been called to Rome to be honored as Masters of Theology. Furthermore, the secretaries of Maryknoll, after a period of being known as "Teresians," had become canonically established as Foreign Mission Sisters of Saint Dominic. Archbishop McNicholas was now offering Maryknoll a new preparatory seminary at Cincinnati, near to his diocesan Seminary of Saint Gregory, from which they could secure instruction. In order to increase the vocations in the Middle West, the preparatory seminary was necessary. Therefore, though it offered a fresh financial burden, Father Walsh in the very thunder of October's catastrophe accepted the offer with eagerness.

"I have never worried," Father Callan heard him say. "Even during distressing times like these, I have not worried, because I have always thought that we were trying to do God's work, and that if we did our part, He would do the rest." [55]

Fortunately the contributors to Maryknoll were almost as little given to gold worship as he was. Their investment in foreign missions had not been prompted by any prospect of financial advantage. Their hearts were not in the stock market. They were comparatively multitudinous and comparatively little impoverished. It was extraordinary how they continued their even handsome gifts. Often the contributions came not attended with the name of any individual; they were gifts of the sodalities and guilds of hundreds of parishes. They were also individual gifts from the thousand relatives and friends of his missioners, people who had given their all, even their brothers, sons, sisters, and daughters, and could not help giving more. Through *The Field Afar,* or even more directly, they were living the lives of those dear to them. They had become conscious of China and Korea, as the French Catholics had been conscious of their missioners and martyred missioners in China, Japan, and Indo-China. The contributors to Maryknoll continued their help.

Father Walsh was not even afraid of making them afraid by disclosing the necessity he was in. He advertised that he wanted seven hundred dollars a year for each missioner—a dollar a day for support and a dollar for the mission work. He asked unabashed for what he needed. It was a way of showing respect for his contributors, and also for the dignity of the missions. Every Catholic, he insisted, should as a Catholic be concerned with foreign missions, and thankful to be able to help them, and he continued to ask. And he asked calmly:

"Maryknoll is usually abreast of the times—up or down—in touch, as it were, with the national life. Consequently, in these days of depression, we feel justly entitled to take our place with the other mourners attending good Dame Fortune's funeral.

"But thanks to God's Providence, we at the Center and our preparatory colleges in this country are still able to carry on.

But where we do mind the pinch is in what comes in, or does not come in, for the foreign-mission field. . . . However, God knows better than we what is best for men's souls; His Church, too, has always made most progress where progress was most difficult. Though, from our human point of view, we regret what seems to be 'marking time,' we are confident that, if we do not fail to do our part, God's work will develop as He desires." [56]

It was his financial salvation that he had never used "high-pressure salesmanship" in driving for funds. He had never relied on emotion, and now, when emotions had so changed, he could still rely on what he had relied on before, a quiet confidence based on a sense of comprehension and intimacy. Through the photographs published in *The Field Afar,* a hundred and fifty thousand readers knew what Maryknoll looked like. They knew that now there was a statue of Our Lady of Maryknoll, Queen of Apostles, in the quadrangle where took place the departure ceremonies. Over her head had been built an Oriental baldachin. Small architectural embellishments like that gave them the sense that Maryknoll was going on, just as the sun was going on, circling the earth, making the dawn. Maryknoll was not folding up like an over-inflated "business." Among other things, its Maryknoll Sisters were increasing and they needed a proper Motherhouse even as an economy. *The Field Afar* needed a proper office, also as an economy. The friends of Maryknoll were frankly and optimistically made acquainted with these needs.

They had confidence in the leaders of Maryknoll, not because they had been pictured as supermen, but because they were so human. Books had, by Maryknollers, been written about Maryknollers. Father Patrick J. Byrne had written a life of Father Price. Bishop James E. Walsh, of Kongmoon, had written a life of Father McShane. And all these lives—as indeed all the letters and articles in *The Field Afar*—contained homely details. Everyone knew, for instance, the legends of Father Price and his rosary. His prayerfulness was if anything exaggerated. He became known as a saint is known, by one special symbol, in his case a rosary—just as if he did not preach at times, and help in administration most ably.

Father Walsh had become known in a different way, partly from accounts of him in *The Field Afar,* when he was referred to as Father Walsh of Boston—as all the missioners were designated as coming, not from nowhere or from anywhere, but from some definite region, just like anyone else—partly from his own way of writing, but also from being seen. He was a man whom even a casual fellow traveler could not forget, for the significant reason that the traveler felt that he himself would not be forgotten, so perfectly had Father Walsh given him for five or ten minutes, or only for one minute, complete attention.

One other factor in making people far and wide feel intimate with Maryknollers and Maryknoll's leaders was photographs. Photography was a variety of journalism for which Father Walsh had the greatest respect. There are readers who never read, as the tabloid newspapers have since discovered, but who look at pictures. To catch such readers, Father Walsh had had the good fortune to enlist among his Maryknollers Father Cotta, who, because his symbol was a kodak as Father

Price's was a rosary, was known as "Father Foto." He was a tall man, around whose neck, like the albatross on the Ancient Mariner, hung a kodak. He could take pictures without seeming to take them. He had the eye of an artist and the mischief of a boy, and he caught the Maryknollers even off-guard. He showed the world what Maryknoll looked like when it did not know it was being looked at. He could "take" Maryknollers who were laughing because they thought someone else was being "taken." Most of his Maryknollers were shown smiling. But why not? *"In camera veritas,"* as the Latin goes.

In 1931 Father Walsh visited his missioners in the far field, whom he knew to be somewhat straitened. Perhaps fortunately they could not imagine what strange goings-on were happening in their homeland; otherwise they would have felt more straitened. The visit, in spite of their predicament, was to him a most consoling one. Never had he imagined that such a change could have taken place. Six years ago, on his preceding visit, the Maryknollers had been taking hold. Now they were established. They were at home. They were as much at home as the European missioners—Lazarists, Jesuits, Dominicans, Franciscans, and Paris missioners—who had seemed such accomplished veterans to him on his first visit, in 1918. They knew the languages; they knew Oriental ways. Visiting his Maryknollers in the Philippines, Korea, Manchuria, and China was like visiting his own homes. They had chapels, dispensaries, schools, and seminaries for the training of native priests, that were not grandiose, not grand even, but comely. They fitted into the landscape as he had hoped they would. They were, after his heart, Maryknolls.

He found that he himself was fitting into China, and in such a strange manner. One day it was by entering Father Ford's prefecture in Kaying, escorted like a local potentate by a cavalry corps of Maryknollers, eight strong, on horseback, he himself in a sedan chair, and then, to make the incongruous still more incongruous, three other Maryknollers, outriders on bicycles. He commented to himself with satisfaction that there were "a larger number of American missioners in that corner of the Kaying field than a score of years ago could have been found in the whole great land of China." [57]

The extent of Maryknoll's activities aroused in him a proud wonder. His former student, James E. Walsh, now Bishop in Kongmoon, was receiving him into a diocese which was so wide that he traveled in a fortnight over a thousand miles in it, and visited eighteen missions.

The Maryknollers were following much the same methods as the French. If they differed from them at all, it was not so much in methods as in spirit. The French, through long experience, were the more astute. The Americans, through almost no experience, were the more intrepid. The French were old. The new recruits that they had looked for to carry on what they had started, had largely been denied them by the anticlerical laws of France in the early nineteen hundreds. The Americans were as young as schoolboys, and recruits as young as they were thronging to their aid.

The American Protestant missioners in the Far East, backed by their very great wealth, had been particularly enterprising in establishing hospitals and colleges. The French and other Europeans, with their much-less-sufficient funds, had not established so many such institutions, and gave to the superficial gaze the impression of not being so much interested in such things. So much so, that to the Chinese the unit of a Catholic mission was the mission compound with its church, and the unit of the Protestant was the hospital.

Father Walsh was not at all disposed to be scornful of the missionary utility of hospitals. Americans—Catholics and Protestants—were identified with the humanitarian work of hospitals, and Maryknoll was disposed to be just as American as any Protestant, where it helped God's work so to be. He had long wished he had some of the hospitals that the Protestants had.

"If we get Catholics in Wuchow," he had commented in 1926, "and they need hospital attendance, we can send them only to the Baptist Hospital. This by the way, according to the doctor's statement, was more than self-supporting last year. I believe that the time has come when we can arouse in American Catholic doctors, nurses, and hospital directors an interest in the mission field, and its splendid opportunity of service for Christ and for the suffering men, women, and children of China." [58]

He had made efforts to develop a hospital service connected with Maryknoll. For ten years the Maryknoll Sisters had been, some of them, becoming real physicians. Likewise some of the Brothers had studied something more than "first aid," as had also every missionary priest. Just recently Maryknoll had sent a professional doctor to China, Doctor Blaber, a volunteer from Brooklyn, who worked with the Maryknollers at Tungon in South China, although not as one of their Society. Now in this year 1931, Father Walsh observed the medical develop-

QUADRANGLE OF MARYKNOLL SEMINARY, IN WHICH EACH YEAR THE DEPARTURE CEREMONY TAKES PLACE

ment with satisfaction, recalling a saying of his: "Every Catholic hospital is a threshold of conversions and a vestibule to heaven." [59]

At the same time, just how far he should spend the talents and funds of Maryknoll in a medical direction remained with him a question. Should he, with so much scantier funds than the Protestants, try to expand his medical work or not? It was asking a good deal of men like Doctor Blaber to expect them to stay for a long period of time in the solitude of interior China. The ideal situation would be to have Catholic hospitals with properly trained Catholic Chinese physicians. But how to arrive at that situation?

Yes, there were questions raised by the Maryknoll success. But for the most part his mind continued to be dominated by happy surprise. Surprise came to him not only from beholding the Maryknollers in China, but from seeing what other American Catholics were doing there. China had been invaded by a score of American groups, stemming from the United States: Dominicans, Passionists, Vincentians, Benedictines, members of the Congregation of the Holy Cross, Franciscans, Salvatorians, Missioners of Saint Columban, and members of the Society of the Divine Word. Not all of them were men—far from it: there were Sisters of Providence, Franciscan Missionaries of Mary, Sisters of Charity, Sisters of the Precious Blood, Religious of the Sacred Heart, Sisters of Notre Dame—American groups of them all.

Of these groups, the Chinese Mission Society of Saint Columban was almost a contemporary of Maryknoll. Five years after Maryknoll's foundation, it had been founded in Ireland, at Maynooth. It had—as already recounted—established itself also in the United States, and was flourishing in almost as many numbers in China. He could rejoice in this twin.

He could rejoice most especially in the Catholic University of Peking (or, as it was now called, Peiping), for his first glimpse of it took away his breath. He had known of it as we know of things we read about. Indeed, it had been just beginning in 1926, when he had last visited China. It was a foundation which had been entrusted to American Benedictines. The autonomy of individual Benedictine houses made it difficult for Benedictines to support and staff a university, and they would shortly have to hand the University of Peiping over to the Society of the Divine Word; but there is no doubt about what they accomplished to begin with. Part of their success had been due to their ability to befriend Chinese art, and to develop a Chinese Christian artistry with the brush and pencil. As outward conspicuous symbol of their success in this field stood their University buildings, which were a monument of architectural art, competing with his Seminary at Maryknoll as an adaptation of the Occident to the Orient. A talented Benedictine, Dom Adelbert Gresnigt, had been the happy architect. And in the buildings were studying, perfectly at home, seven hundred Chinese young men.

It was amazing what American Catholics were doing after so few years having elapsed since they had done almost nothing. The collections of the United States for the S.P.F. had quadrupled. The various diocesan offices of the S.P.F., throughout the nation, were collecting over two million dollars a year. The United States was now the chief contributor to the S.P.F.

There was always a danger of nationalism creeping into missionary endeavor. It was partly to obviate this that Pope Benedict XV had transferred the seat of the S.P.F. from Lyons to Rome. There might now be a danger to Father Walsh in taking too great an American pride in America's part. But no, it was not so much America's feat that astonished him as the wonder of Providence which had invited America to her missionary destiny just in time for both China's difficulties and Europe's. All missionary activity in the Orient seemed to be under Providence's special favor.

"The marvel is—and it grows on me whenever I visit the Orient—that the Catholic Church has accomplished what she has there, with the measure of alms that she has received from Europe and America. Faith and sacrifice have doubtless made up for what was wanting materially. God supplies when man fails." [60]

Speaking of the Catholic University at Peiping, he thanked Divine Providence even more than the Benedictines: "How all this has been accomplished in a few years is little short of a miracle. Evidently God wanted it done, and that is how its organizers feel about it—just as we do about Maryknoll." [61]

There had come into existence by this time, largely through the generosity of Mr. George McDonald, K.S.G., a "procure" for Maryknoll at Hong Kong, which served as a Maryknoll hostel, rest house, and retreat house. From it Father Walsh wrote several letters home to Maryknoll. In one he congratulated Maryknollers in having their Maryknoll on Sunset Hill:

"Homesteads disappear in our country, and many a boy will recall only a succession of flats—as the base of his childhood memories.

"We children of the Church are more fortunate, because the Church builds for generations to come. Maryknoll has such a Center. May it be for each of its sons an inspiration and joyful memory!

"I keep you in my poor prayers; keep me in your good ones." [62]

In another letter he gave more thought to the departure Maryknollers would one day make from Maryknoll:

"During these past long weeks in South China, I have written rarely but I have thought frequently of you all, and I have not failed to offer prayers for you.

"You are preparing for such a life as I have been observing, and I wish that you could visualize, even remotely, the conditions, favorable and unfavorable, which a missioner in the Orient will necessarily meet.

"You hear letters and diaries read as did your predecessors, but the impression left is often light, or colored by the imagination, or clouded by preconceived notions, if not lost altogether; so that when you cross the ocean you will find yourselves, to a considerable extent, strangers to the new life and confronted with experience unrealized if not unknown. So be it! This lack of observation will not prevent the continued exercise of the generosity that started and brought you into the service of Christ. Your offering of self has been 'all for all,' and you are being tested, but the great test will be met when you leave the home nest.

"I cannot urge you too strongly—in these days of preparation—to watch and *scotch* any tendency to lower your apostolic ideal.

"Keep generous; forget self and be thoughtful of others; work perseveringly; be miserly with time; seek criticism rather than make it; and recall often that daily self-denial is expected from a follower of Christ.

"Pray for me. I hope to see you soon." [63]

By June's end he was back in Maryknoll, after having crossed a country, from the Pacific to the Atlantic, which was miserable with unemployment, and bewilderment, and resentment against Europe for the debts which allies and former foes there were failing to pay. Was this land in a mood to continue its work in the Far East, which was just beginning to show its fruitfulness?

God bless the recruits! They at least were swarming. In September Maryknoll reopened with a record attendance of theologians at the major Seminary and of junior students at the preparatories. He commented in *The Field Afar:*

"Some might not consider the present period of economic depression a time when a large increase in 'the family' would bring happiness; but we are confident that the Master who has called these generous young souls to His service in the fields afar will inspire in other hearts the desire to aid us in their training." [64]

He had confidence in the "other hearts"; also he had confidence in his Maryknoll missioners at the world's end. He admonished them:

"We have been struggling during this period of financial distress against a greatly reduced income, that has necessitated our borrowing to meet current expenses.

"God is good, and we marvel at the charity of the faithful in spite of the depression.

"We must work, however, and the time has come for us to call on every Maryknoll priest, Brother, and student, to help us pull through a difficult period.

"We, therefore, pledge ourselves individually to do what we can; and we ask you to find among your friends one hundred dollars for the needs of the Society—one hundred subscribers to *The Field Afar,* or two perpetual memberships, or stringless gifts.

"In the meantime, we suggest special prayers for our increasing needs." [65]

Maryknoll would go on. It would have to go on.

"I am well aware that we have a growing number of pagans in this country; and that, if they can be won from a worship of material things to serve the living God, a mighty task will have been accomplished. The Christian has a duty towards these people, but not to the exclusion of those who have never had the advantage of contact with the Spirit of Christ.

"For the Awakened Orient this is the hour when ageless culture is disintegrating, and nations suffering the pangs of rebirth need all that we can give to counteract the deadening poison of Sovietism and the flippant sophistication of the Western World." [66]

But in order to go on, Maryknoll must remember that there is a spiritual ladder ever to be climbed:

"Perhaps He expects more from us—more real patience, purer motives, more charity, greater forbearance, more thoughtfulness; less striving after natural satisfaction, less complaint about our conditions, less insistence on material means. Our riches are the riches of faith. These, with the love of God, a spirit of sacrifice and earnest prayer, will attract souls though we lack in material help what we think is needful. *Primum Regnum Dei.* . . . . We can only do our best with what we have and leave results to God." [67]

One of the things that had ever given encouragement to Father Walsh had been the development of the congregation of Maryknoll Sisters. It had come about almost without his planning. The various steps in the evolution of the secretaries into religious Sisters had taken place as if from an internal principle within the group, and had called for his approval and ordering only after they had in fact happened. The vocations to the Maryknoll Sisterhood were more numerous than the vocations to his own Society. It was encouraging now, in this year 1932, to see how they were prospering. It was in 1929 that Bishop Dunn had broken the ground for a Motherhouse for them on land which was really theirs. In the spring of 1932, they had occupied this Motherhouse, across the road from the Seminary.

Their vigorous autonomy which enabled them to set up for themselves filled him with admiration. At the same time the fact that they were able to quit their overcrowded buildings on his land, and leave them vacant for other purposes, was a convenience to him. One of the buildings—Saint Joseph's— could be used by him as a novitiate for his Maryknollers. It was almost as if the Sisters were cutting a furrow ahead of him, in which he could follow.

It was not necessary that his Maryknoll men be great theologians or speculative mystics, but it was necessary that they be men of prayer, so many graces did they need. The fact that they were called to a life of action made their prayerfulness all the more necessary. Constant prayer, however, they could not give themselves to. They had had to rely for constant prayer at one time on the Carmelites. But now, in the fall of 1932, the Maryknoll Sisters found themselves able to give this help of unintermittent prayer.

For some years Mother Mary Joseph and he had dreamed that a portion of the community of Sisters might be set aside for a purely contemplative life. And now with the opening of the Motherhouse, the achievement of this dream was made possible. There was a farmhouse on the Sisters' property, on the very height of their land, called *Regina Coeli* House, which they turned into a special house of prayer. Into it entered a dozen Maryknoll Sisters who felt a call to contemplation. On the Feast of Saint Francis of Assisi, October 4, 1932, these Sisters of Saint Dominic—Saint Francis's sweet rival—were with due ceremony enclosed in *Regina Coeli* Cloister by Bishop Dunn, who on the same day had consecrated the altar in the Motherhouse chapel. Thus Maryknoll was in every way becoming complete. Firmly planted on earth, it was towering to heaven, with a Jacob's Ladder that reached to heaven's door.

So Maryknoll, instead of becoming a ruin, continued to grow. It was one of the few things in the United States that, flourishing in the 1920's, flourished just as much in the 1930's.

"To all I reiterate—more strongly than ever—that God's arm is not shortened. So far, He has made it possible for the Society to provide every missioner with food and shelter, travel and other necessary expenses—and to secure occasional substantial help for the missions, besides sustaining in large measure the several student bodies in this country, and meeting heavy interest obligations.

"We are often asked how we can do it, and the only answer is found in God's Providence, responding to man's activity." [68]

Towards the end of 1932, the banks in the United States, even the strongest of them, began to wobble. Father Walsh did not wobble. During the presidential election of 1932, when Franklin Roosevelt was campaigning against Herbert Hoover, and when there was almost complete uneasiness everywhere, he was negotiating with Cardinal O'Connell of Boston for the foundation of a novitiate in the Boston Archdiocese. His sense of the heroic virtues required of his missioners in a period of stringency, convinced him that heroic virtues had to be in every way developed in them. As early as 1929 he had decided that, when feasible, a year between "philosophy" and "theology" should be set aside for a special spiritual training. It was something that his own missioners in China had counseled him to do. So, as soon as the removal of the Sisters to their own new Motherhouse had been accomplished, he had instituted a novitiate in one of these buildings. But it was recognized that a greater remoteness from the general activities of Maryknoll would be more appropriate for these novices. Hence he turned to the Boston Archdiocese as a possible site. At Bedford, thirty miles from Boston on the Concord River, stood a farm which had for some time belonged to the Brighton Seminary as a furnisher of supplies. It was hoped that Cardinal O'Connell would be willing to part with this farm. And he was—and he sold it to Maryknoll for a price which amounted to a gift. The deed was signed in November.

On March 4, 1933, President Franklin Delano Roosevelt was inaugurated. On March 7 he proclaimed a "holiday" for the banks in the United States, as indeed he absolutely had to do. For a week they remained closed. It was very disquieting. But Father Walsh was neither disquieted nor wishfully optimistic —not in merely economic affairs. He visited Bedford during April's last week. Irrespective of depressions, he was going on with his novitiate. There must be no spiritual depression. A barn at Bedford was being turned into a dormitory.

Most of Father Walsh's intimate friends, aside from his own family, dated from his seminary days in Saint John's, Brighton. A few dated from his early years in the priesthood. Thus Boston contained most of his boon companions, who knew him not so much as the Superior General of Maryknoll, but rather as their own inimitable comrade and wit. One of his particular boon companions was Father James F. Kelly, who had journeyed with him to the East—and then back by way of Rome—in 1921. Father Kelly was pastor of the Church of Our Lady of Lourdes in an outlying district of Boston, Jamaica Plain. He was building for his parish a new church, and in that particular kind of audacity which consists in daring what Providence suggests was a confrere of Father Walsh. On April 24, after a day at Bedford, Father Walsh dined with Father Kelly.

They had eaten their dinner. They were sitting with the

parish curates, refusing to worry about anything. Father Kelly was not worrying about the wherewithal for his new parish church; Father Walsh was not worrying about the rising expenses of Maryknoll.

The evening was a happy one, when the door bell—most unhappy sound—unwelcomely rang. Steps outside. In came a member of Maryknoll's Council, looking a little lugubrious. Then an interval—then another. Another—still another. Each looked appropriately more lugubrious than the preceding, like the descending notes in a scale of music. Father Walsh was bent on not being worried, but to find himself thus overtaken by four of his henchmen, all of them unresponsive to his cheery salutations to them, cast a shadow over his spirits, a shadow of the unknown. They had followed him from the Hudson River to Jamaica Pond, three hundred miles, for something. And yet they were loath to divulge anything. They just looked gloom, like Cassius quadruplets come to murder their Caesar, and ready to do it without joy, in a sense of duty. They had never had this appearance before.

Finally they began, or their spokesman began: "Father General, we have received advice from Rome—it seems we are making a mistake, a very grave mistake. The mistake is—" and here he paused as if some calamity were unspeakable—"the mistake is, that we are calling you Father General, whereas, *Your Excellency,* it should be *Bishop* General. And we, the Council, offer you our heartiest felicitations!" [69]

The Bishop

IT TURNED out that a cable had arrived at Maryknoll from Rome on the very morning of the day—April 24, 1933—when Father Walsh was to dine with Father Kelly. It had brought the unexpected news that Maryknoll's Superior was to be raised to the episcopacy as Titular Bishop of Siene; whereupon Maryknoll's Council, in the best car they could commandeer, had sped across Connecticut and Massachusetts, past meadows beginning to show their spring green, and past green willows, and under maples in red blossom, to announce the tidings to their Superior.

Now they had found him. His eyebrows were arched, as they always were, in anticipated surprise, so that he scarcely needed to change the expression of his face at hearing the news. All that he had to do was to sit back in his chair (which did not resemble a bishop's chair), and smile at the joke which had been played on him by the lugubrious faces of his Maryknoll Councilors. Interiorly he was more prepared for bad news than good—so much so that he was leaning the wrong way to receive the shock of what was told him. Yes, it was a shock, although a blessing. For the first time during the depression, he was confronted with a situation for which he was unprepared, and consequently now at last he was perturbed.

"I have never cared for these things," he murmured. "I have never had any particular taste for rings, or miters, or crosiers, or purple robes, or flowing vestments. I honor these things in others, and I know that they hold a sacred place in the hierarchy and in the work of the Church; but I have never cared for them for myself, because I always feared they would interfere with and hamper my lifework. But of course I am getting to be an old man now, and perhaps it won't matter." [70]

Yet here was the hand of God; and, for all his perturbation, he was very quiet at the news, recalling to himself that it was an honor to Maryknoll rather than to himself, and that the emotions should be Maryknoll's, not his.

His consecration would take place at Rome on June 29, the Feast of Saints Peter and Paul, which was the twenty-second anniversary of the day in 1911, when Cardinal Gotti, Prefect of the Sacred Congregation of Propaganda, had given Father Walsh and Father Price authorization to start their Seminary.

It was well ahead of time, on June 2, that he started for Rome from New York with Maryknoll's Father Keller. He wanted to be in Rome with enough free days before his consecration, so that he could make what material preparations were necessary, and also seclude himself in a six-day retreat. That was one reason for the early sailing date. Another reason may have been the convenience of choosing this or that steamer. But there was still another reason: there was to be held at Rome, on June 11, a ceremony so significant that he wished to be present at it. It was to be another consecration, more important to his eyes—and, so it seemed, to the eyes of the Holy Father, who at it was to act as consecrator—than his own consecration. It was the raising to the episcopate of five native priests from the Orient—three of them natives of China, one of them of India, one other of Indo-China.

No one of these priests had ever been instructed by missioners from Maryknoll. They had nothing to do with Maryknoll directly, yet symbolically they in their consecration stood for the goal of Maryknoll. Maryknoll did not hope or aspire to convert the hundreds of millions of China—not by itself. Its goal was rather to establish in China the Church with its native clergy, so that the conversion of the hundreds of millions could be accomplished by the Chinese themselves. It was with this goal in mind that Maryknoll's vicars apostolic had set up in their vicariates, as soon as the vicariates could support them, seminaries for the education of native priests. Already in China and Korea, Maryknoll had two hundred seminarians. Bishop James E. Walsh, who was himself the first native-born American Bishop to be consecrated on Chinese soil, had in the preceding June ordained two native Chinese of Kongmoon, two of his seminarians, to the priesthood. Now these other five native priests who had been trained originally by missioners—not Maryknollers—in the Far East, were to present in their consecration a picture of the future of which Maryknoll dreamed, and for which Maryknollers were now, like other Christs, sacrificing themselves.

Father Walsh arrived in Rome for the consecration on June 11. He even arrived a day ahead of time. When he was present at it, he gazed at it with such a concentration that it seemed his whole life was looking at it, out through his eyes. He had forgotten himself. After that he could wait for his own cere-

mony, could wait unexalted, unexultant, for it, and quietly. On
June 22 he wrote a letter back to Maryknoll:

"It seems like an age since I left Maryknoll—where time
actually flies for me when I am there.

"I have been in Rome since June 10 (12 days)—and have
just completed preparations for the consecration. Also I have
had my first audience with the Holy Father. . . .

"I feel that I shall have some good Maryknoll prayers this
week, and I will do my best to return the spiritual favor. I
must think much on my device—*Primum Regnum Dei*—lest
having preached to others I myself become, if not a castaway,
at least a fit subject for criticism. I see so much to be improved
in myself and in the many features of our work.

"When I thanked the Holy Father for the honor of the
episcopate and for his confidence, he replied: 'Don't thank me.
Thank God. We are only His instruments.'

"I plan to leave Genoa by the *Rex,* July 12, arriving at New
York July 19. Pray me home safe, and expect a triple blessing."

On June 25 he wrote an even more quiet letter to his
nephew Jack, son of his sister, Mrs. Hughes:

"I am writing from the Jesuit retreat house on the Janiculum Hill, with the dome of Saint Peter's in view on one
side, the Tiber and the city proper on the other. A palm tree is
outside of my door, which serves also as a window; and, as
the building is on a hillside, there are several small terraces
that provide gardens for an occasional saunter. An elevator to
the roof gives me an occasional recreation and a fine view that
at night is something of a dream.

"I came here last Thursday evening. I shall be here until
Wednesday morning, and after a Jubilee visit to the great

basilicas, I will return to our own Maryknoll house and make final preparations for the consecration ceremony, which will be held Thursday morning at eight, at the chapel of the new Propaganda College, which I can see whenever I go to the roof these days. The college is just above us, and it is interesting to watch the students of all colors and nationalities as they pass to their classes or play at recreation.

"I have written no letters since coming here, but I am making an exception for you as I think of you finishing your college course and beginning your adult life—or shall I call it your struggle with the world? You have done well to have reached this milestone in your career, clean, obedient and loyal to your Christian heritage. The close of this period in your life marks a new beginning, but it leaves you with a foundation that is capable of carrying a fine structure.

"I don't know what will be your lifework, and perhaps you do not know yourself, but I urge you these days to say a frequent prayer to the Holy Ghost for light, and keep eyes and ears open for suggestions or inspiration. Your success so far has come because you worked well, and what success lies before you will also be in proportion to the efforts you make. It is only the man who works that can accomplish.

"If you take up some business enterprise, as you have been considering, you will find it valuable, even necessary, to meet people who under other conditions might not appeal to you as worth-while cultivating. Among these will be some of sterling qualities, others whose business ability far exceeds their qualities of mind and heart. We influence one another, and my advice to students has always been to select as companions

BISHOP WALSH OFFICIATES AT THE DEPARTURE
CEREMONY OF MARYKNOLL MISSIONERS FOR THE
FAR EAST

those who are better than themselves, so as gradually to rise to higher standards and ideals."

Now the day of his consecration was impending. All was arranged. The successor to Cardinal Gotti, Cardinal Fumasoni-Biondi, would be the consecrator. There would be, as always, two other coconsecrators: one would be Archbishop McNicholas of Cincinnati; the other would be Bishop Dunn, Auxiliary Bishop of New York, who was conducting a pilgrimage from New York for the nineteen-hundredth anniversary of Our Lord's Crucifixion.

There is something extraordinary in being a bishop in this life of ours which the Devil does his level best to make appear level and commonplace. There is something even perceptibly extraordinary in a bishop, as a proof of which one has only to observe the stir and the turning of heads that the arrival of any bishop makes in any gathering. It is not the color which he wears that makes the impression through the eye. Nor can it be easily said which of our senses perceives that a bishop is a bishop. It would seem that God has cast an aura about bishops, which the little grace we have can perceive, or even our hatred of grace. A bishop emaciated, mutilated, in rags, in a soviet concentration camp, is visibly a bishop.

It is only appropriate, therefore, that the consecration of a bishop should be an event extraordinary, awesome, apocalyptic, and audacious, beyond any mere earthly ceremony or etiquette. We have all heard that the raising of a priest to the episcopate is but a conferring on him of the "fullness of the priesthood." In other words, his consecration is but a continuation of his ordination. There is no new sacrament involved. But the "fullness of the priesthood" is a phrase of tremendous meaning: it confers all the status on the recipient that the Holy Father himself possesses, for the Holy Father is but the Bishop first among bishops. Thus the consecration is not a mere ornate addition to the ceremony of ordination. It is not a rite to please the eye and to flatter the recipient by presenting him with a title and handsome gifts—a crosier, a ring, a miter, and gloves. It is not the pomp of consecration that impresses the beholder. Rather, it is the simplicity of it.

The bishop-elect is not personally exalted by the ceremony. Scarcely ever in his life since baptism has he been treated so as a child. As Father Manasses P. Dougherty, in Saint Peter's at Cambridge, had asked of the sponsors of Mr. James Walsh's son James, "What dost thou demand?" so the consecrating bishop demands of two coconsecrating bishops as they present their bishop-elect, "Have you the Apostolic Mandate?"

"We have," is their answer. Then the bishop-elect is examined like a schoolboy.

Question: "Will you teach the people for whom you are ordained, both by words and by example, the things you understand from the divine Scriptures?"

Answer: "I will."

Question: "Will you yourself observe, and likewise teach others to observe, humility and patience?"

Answer: "I will."

As the ceremony goes on, the bishop-elect is treated even more as a child. He is dressed by others as if he were a babe. The ceremonies are as direct as if they were invented by a child, the Divine Child—the Infant of Prague—to be seen and understood by other children not divine. Three bishops lay their hands on his helpless head.

"Receive the Holy Spirit."

"Receive the Holy Spirit."

"Receive the Holy Spirit."

Before he can touch the Evangel, the book is opened and set upon him as if he had no hands. It is made to rest on his shoulders and bent head, even for a long time, as if its weight and meaning should enter into him.

Then come the appropriate gifts: gloves, which express respect for holy things; a ring, which symbolizes the spiritual alliance contracted by the bishop toward the Church of which he is pastor; a miter, which recalls the two rays of light which lit the face of Moses when he stood before God on Sinai; and the crosier, which is the shepherd's crook, curved to seize and bring back his sheep, with staff and point expressive of firmness and vigilance.

The whole ceremony is calculated to impress on the bishop-elect that he is becoming even more fully God's instrument. It recalls the creation of Adam out of the earth's clay. It is, I believe, in connection with a consecration of a bishop that the play on words, so easy in the Latin, that the honor is more "onerous" than "honoring," has had the longest life. Never anywhere in the wording of the rite is there the slightest suggestion that the bishop-elect is being rewarded for past services.

It is the consecrating of the bishop that confers the "onus." It is only the choosing him to be consecrated that confers the honor. The honor for Father Walsh was double, for in his case there was no necessity of choosing anybody. Over a regular diocese it is necessary to have a bishop. Otherwise there can be no ordination of priests, no confirmation, no blessing of oils and chrisms, no dedication of churches. Over a missionary region—a vicariate, or even a prefecture—it is almost impossible not to have a bishop, or one with some of the faculties of the bishop. Therefore Maryknoll had had one bishop in the Orient, and three prefects apostolic who could in their regions act somewhat as bishops. But Maryknoll on the Hudson had no children to confirm, and its chapels could be dedicated by a bishop of the diocese in which they stood. To choose a man to be made bishop at Maryknoll was a singularly free act, actuated by no necessity to make any choice whatsoever. The chooser—the Holy Father—was being constrained merely by a sense of what was appropriate in God's economy.

The choice was a tribute to the missionary activity of the United States. Fifteen years before this, when Maryknoll's contingent of four was preparing to start for the East, a list of missionary activities emanating from the various nations of Christendom would, after the name of the United States, have left a blank. Now it was different. The French still led in the number of missioners—thirty-three hundred. The Italians were second with twelve hundred; the Belgians third. Then came the Germans, Hollanders, and Spaniards. The Americans came near the end of the list with three hundred and seventy-three. Father Walsh was not alone responsible for the Americans. But he was largely responsible for Maryknoll, and Maryknoll had over a hundred and twenty missioners at work.

Maryknoll showed, moreover, great promise for the future. It had two hundred and sixty-five students preparing to go to the Far East. It had sixty-eight Auxiliary Brothers ready to help them. As allies it had four hundred and fifty-seven Sisters of Saint Dominic. In giving recognition to this missionary movement, which had burst with such suddenness, it was inevitable to turn to the Superior General of Maryknoll and single him out as symbol of the movement.

The episcopacy stands for permanence. Without bishops a priesthood is unperpetuating. Because of bishops the Church has gone on since the days of Christ, and only through bishops can it continue until the end of time. To elevate the Superior of Maryknoll to the episcopate was to badge Maryknoll and all the mission endeavor of the United States with permanency. Thus the consecration of James Anthony Walsh as Bishop was to be an act of confidence in the future of the United States.

Thus the consecration of Bishop-elect Walsh was to be the great day in his life. It was the setting of a visible seal of approbation on his life's work. He could not escape from feeling it as such, for he had only to note the cloud of earthly witnesses that were present at the event. From Boston had come his brother Timothy, the architect; and Father James F. Kelly, whom the Chinese had called *Father Kay;* and his other companion in visiting the East, Father Crane; and Father Bruneau, SS., once of Boston.

The chapel of the Propaganda College, the Urban College —the new college on the Janiculum, behind the Vatican—was to be the scene of the consecration.

The *Fides Service,* which Father Considine had helped start, described the event as follows:

"The morning of June twenty-ninth dawned threatening, but broke clear and crystal bright. New Rome beamed in loveliness, sang with its bells and its fountains. The new Urban College, built for the Holy See through the special assistance of the Archdiocese of Chicago, stood superbly amid its green gardens on the Janiculum Hill and played the host.

"America climbed to the eminence overlooking Saint Peter's in the persons of some two hundred or more visitors from overseas, laymen and clergy, including priests of Maryknoll and the Mother General of the Maryknoll Sisters, Mother Mary Joseph; in prelates such as Monsignor Duggan, of Hartford, and Monsignor Cashin, of New York; in bishops, among whom were Bishop McNally, of Hamilton, Ontario, and Bishop Vehr, of Denver; in the coconsecrators, Archbishop McNicholas, of Cincinnati, and Bishop Dunn, of New York; and finally the *consecrandus,* thoughtful and uncomforted at the prospect of being this time the center of attention rather than the director of others, yet thoroughly aware of the significance of this ceremony to the cause for which he has given most of his sixty-six years.

"Europe came up the hill in the persons of representatives of many religious communities, dedicated in whole or in part to the missions; and in visitors such as Bishop Fitzgerald, of Gibraltar.

"The mission world came in bearded ambassadors from Asia and Africa; in Archbishop Costantini, Apostolic Delegate to China; and in Archbishop Bernardini, Apostolic Delegate to Australia and Oceania.

"Rome came in the persons of students of many nations from the ecclesiastical colleges; in professors and superiors; in officers of the Congregation of Propaganda and allied bureaus; in prelates such as Archbishop Spolverini and Monsignors Cesarini, Carminati, and Zanin; in princes of the Church in the Vicar of Rome, Cardinal Marchetti-Selvaggiani, and the consecrator, Cardinal Fumasoni-Biondi. It was Rome, indeed, that consecrated; it was from a study in the austere building across the piazza that the successor of Peter had sent forth the call, and now by the hands of the Cardinal Prefect of Propaganda, Rome's representative for mission activities, the dignity would be conferred." [71]

And the evening came, and the great day for the United States and Bishop Walsh was over. Another day momentous for Christendom followed. Since 1870 the Popes had not gone out of their retreat in the Vatican, prisoned there by the world's secularism. But on the day following Bishop Walsh's consecration, the Pope of Missions went forth from his restrictions, in a deed symbolic of his re-emergence into the affairs of the world, and visited the Basilica of the Apostle to the Gentiles, Saint Paul's Outside the Walls.

On the first of July, the new Bishop was received by the Holy Father in private audience. The Pope of the Missions gave to this American organizer of American missions a pectoral cross, which is a usual gift from the Holy Father to any bishop consecrated in Rome—and then he surprised the missioner with another gift:

"And as a mark of special esteem for the cause which you represent, I add this ring."

On Sunday Bishop Walsh began to do what he had not normally been empowered to do before. In the *Collegio Maryknoll,* he administered the Sacrament of Confirmation to a young American convert, Mr. Bernard Peebles, who was studying at the American Academy in Rome.

By July 18 he was back in Maryknoll, a Bishop of Siene, looking again at the vigor of his green-roofed Seminary on Sunset Hill.

The Sufferer

BISHOP WALSH resumed his daily tasks at Maryknoll at a time when nature seemed to be rejoicing at the consummation of so many of his hopes. It was the season of rich greenness, and sunny perfume of sunny flowers. Also it was just in time to preside at the most dramatic of Maryknoll's annual ceremonies, the departure ceremony.

No longer did the ceremony take place in September, and no longer in a small chapel. It took place in the grand quadrangle of the Maryknoll Seminary, in which presided, in an Oriental kiosk, the statue of Our Lady of Maryknoll, Queen of Apostles. Higher than Our Lady, carved into the stone of the façade of the Seminary, hovered perpetually the Dove of the Holy Spirit. It was a quadrangle enclosed on three sides: to the east, to the north, to the west. Only to the south was the sky open down to the horizon, and that horizon was far off, beyond the valley of the Hudson. Between the Seminary and that sky there stood on the terrace edge the yoke-like frame in which hung the once-pagan bell, the summons of which called the missioners to the Orient, which the setting sun made to appear so near—the land of Saint Francis Xavier.

This year there were to be fifteen young men starting for

228

the East: fourteen priests and one Brother. They came, one of them from Cuba City, Wisconsin, and one of them from Cottonwood, Idaho, and one from Connecticut, and one from Pennsylvania, and the others from New York and Massachusetts. They were a present from all over the United States to the entire Orient. Two were bound for Kongmoon in South China; and two to Kaying, South China; and three to Wuchow, South China; and two to Pengyang, Korea; and two to Fushun, Manchukuo; and one to Manila; and three, for the first time, to Japan.

The departure ceremonies were the distinctive event in Maryknoll's years. They distinguished Maryknoll's years from those of diocesan seminaries. They were an affectionate leave-taking. This world is an exile in comparison with heaven. The mission life afar was an exile in comparison with life at home, and the Maryknollers abroad were often in *The Field Afar* referred to as "our exiles." Thus the departure ceremonies emphasized the particular heroism which had to exist in every Maryknoller.

These ceremonies were based on those of the *Rue du Bac,* which had long drawn tears from the stones of Paris. They were in themselves so moving that at them Maryknoll's Superior, who regularly addressed the new exiles, spoke with a calm to allay rather than to arouse emotions. They began with the smiting of the bell, at which the procession of the future exiles emerged. They continued with the murmur and resonance of prayers that echoed ever with words concerning paths and journeys:

"Blessed be the Lord God of Israel; for He hath visited and wrought the redemption of His people. . . . For thou shalt go before the face of the Lord to prepare His ways. To give knowledge of salvation to His people, unto the remission of their sins. . . . To enlighten those who sit in darkness and in the shadow of death."

"Show us Thy paths, O Lord."

"God hath given His angels charge over thee, that they may keep thee in all thy ways."

"O God, who madest the children of Israel to walk with dry feet through the midst of the sea, and who didst open unto the Three Wise Men, by the guiding of a star, the way that led unto Thee, grant us good speed and quietness, that Thy holy angel may be with us, and that we may happily come thither whither we would now, and in the end unto the haven of eternal salvation."

After that came the Superior's address. Then each of the new missioners read his *propositum,* or pledge to remain in the Society for life, and received from the Superior a crucifix.

There followed the singing of the *Veni, Creator Spiritus,* in which with the extraordinary familiarity of Christians (which we take as a matter of course) the Maryknollers asked God the Holy Spirit to be guest in their hearts, giving them eloquence, light, love.

Next came the giving of the *pax* or kiss of peace. First the Superior gave it to each of the missioners, and then past the missioners filed the whole community—priests, students, Brothers—giving and receiving the kiss as a farewell embrace.

After that rose the strains of the Departure Hymn, which had been composed by the French musician, Charles Francois Gounod, the author of the famous music of "Faust," who, aside from writing operas, had at one time in the 1840's been the organist at the mission chapel on the *Rue du Bac,* and who all his life had been deeply stirred—more than by anything else—by the beauty of a missionary vocation. It was a hymn regularly sung by the Paris missioners at their departure ceremonies. It belonged to them. But also now, through Blessed Théophane Vénard, whose relics were at Maryknoll, as well as his memory and his patronage, it was Maryknoll's heritage.

"Go forth, ye heralds of God's tender mercy;
The day has come at last, the day of joy."

So went the English of the hymn, but how in any language could it say what words were no match for?

Our Lady had said the unsayable in her *Magnificat.* It was the *Magnificat* that was next sung. Pinnacle of all hymns, with its reserve, and its emotion above emotion, sung and composed by one who, precursor of missioners, carried her Christ and God under and next her heart over the hills of Judea!

"My soul doth magnify the Lord . . . because He that is mighty hath done great things to me."

The Superior who conducted the departure ceremony in this year 1933 could still hear in his ears the hymns and prayers of his own ceremony of consecration. *"Ad multos annos!"* he had said, according to custom, to his consecrating bishops after they had finished the rite. *"Ad multos annos!*—Long life to you!" And the Maryknollers had echoed the same salutation to him. He could have but one consecration, but the departure ceremonies would recur and recur, and he would be present at them, he the Bishop, to give them continuity. *Ad multos annos!* He was only sixty-six. His daylight of a life need not be considered as nearing an ending.

True, during the departure ceremony he had felt thoroughly exhausted, but that was natural, for he had contracted a feeling of fatigue while in Rome, which unfortunately he had been unable to shake off, even on a sea voyage. The experience of being consecrated is fatiguing, and ought to be recognized as such, and his mere feelings, which tried to whisper to him that a real change was taking place in his health, ought to be disregarded. He had had such feelings before, even in youth. How spent and downhearted he had felt that year, the year before he decided to become a priest! He would not listen to the old-wives' tales told by a mere fable-loving feeling. They were to be discounted.

In August two sad blows fell on him: Father Bruneau died in France, and Bishop Dunn in New York. For his own self, however, he saw not the slightest indication of death. His present fatigue could be cured by the same method that previous fatigues had been cured. Travel, relaxation, an ability that he had to cast off care, could serve as cure-alls.

Least of all did he look forward to leading his bishop's life as an invalid, showing his chief fortitude and activity in resisting the petty woes of an ailing body. He did not imagine himself as entering the vocation of a sufferer. As Bishop he would be a little more active than before, and a little stronger. He was not going to sit back as Superior simply because he wore purple, a thin line of it showing. So far as his Mary-knollers were concerned, he did not even wish to be referred to as Bishop. He was to continue as their Father General, with the accent on the *Father*. In addition he would enjoy a few activities which bind a bishop to his flock. He could not confirm Maryknollers: they were already confirmed. But occasionally he did administer the Sacrament of Confirmation, partly for the joy of being near children and of having a chance to speak to them. And he could ordain at Maryknoll. On September 24, of this year 1933, he ordained three of his priests.

He continued therefore, as before, his active life, trusting that any day the fatigue would fall from his shoulders. Surely it was not a weight that had been impressed on his soul at consecration. During the summer he attended the biennial convention of the Catholic Students' Mission Crusade at Cincinnati, and at it on August 9, 1933, he delivered an address. In it he did not talk like a Nestor, living in the past, and wanting to live more in the past, and making the past seem interminable with accounts of how wonderful the past was. In his discourse he went ahead of his audience into the future.

"Progress, then," he had to acknowledge, "there has been. But we shall be wise to look upon American foreign-mission effort so far rather as a good start."

He impressed upon the students the work of the future— his work and theirs. Only nineteen per cent of the world's population was Catholic. How could any one think that the Catholics of the United States were really awake to foreign missions? "Even yet the proportion of mission-minded American Catholics is small." These students had the task of waking them up. These students had everything to do.

Only once did he give the slightest hint that he had any apprehension that he, thinking so of the future, might not be with them long in the future. It was when he said: "Some never live to gather the fruit of their seeding. 'Do your best, and leave results to God.' " But even then he may not have been thinking of himself in particular.

He was, however, in particular still doing his best. He would not relinquish his old habit of being a busy correspondent, even in his own handwriting. The morning after the meeting, while lodged in the house of the Dominican and friendly Archbishop McNicholas, he penned a letter to his two Dominican professors at Maryknoll:

"This is a line to thank you both for the kind reception and generous offering which I received last Sunday. We all enjoyed the visit.

"I came here yesterday in time to address the Students' Mission Crusade last evening.

"Some 32 dioceses are represented here, with 400 delegates outside of Cincinnati. This is a promising movement, which ought to help the mission cause at home and abroad." [72]

In the subsequent November he was able to go busily to the opening of the novitiate at Bedford in the Boston Archdiocese. It was Cardinal O'Connell who blessed the new building, and Cardinal O'Connell who made the chief address. But Bishop Walsh was there, nimble in mind, recalling in gratitude the early encouragement that Cardinal O'Connell had given him, and planning for the future as youthfully as ever.

And he passed through the winter rejoicing to be a bishop, and visiting as a bishop all his seminaries and schools and procures in the land, giving them, as is a bishop's custom, a holiday, as if he were a boy liking to interrupt studies.

On the seventeenth of June, 1934, he ordained eighteen of his young men. He could hardly stand up to finish the rite, but only his intimates perceived his condition. On July 7 he heard the news of his brother Timothy's death. He had one sister still alive—Mrs. Hughes—but otherwise, father, mother, brothers, sisters were all dead. But it did not mean that his own fatigue was mortal.

He planned cheerfully to visit his missioners in the Far East, but here his doctors stepped in. They advised him that it would be well for him to postpone such exertions. He was needed, and he must have health in order to continue. It would be well for him to return to Europe, this time for a rest. So far as his health was concerned, the main object of his crossing was a visit to Wörishofen in Bavaria for a treatment, a part of which amused him immensely—his having by doctor's order to go about without socks—and all of which he took with a vein of humor.

But it was nearer to his heart to visit places more spiritual: Oberammergau; Konnersreuth, the home of Therese Neumann; Lisieux, the home of Saint Therese the Little; and Nevers. There was little of touristing in these visits. For some years he had heard of the apparently supernatural sufferings of the stigmatic Therese Neumann, and he happened to know Friederick Ritter von Lama, who had written about them. The latter had impressed him as a man to be trusted, and his story was unbelievably touching. He was touched more than he expected to be by his real meeting with Therese; she was so simple, straightforward, and nobly peasant-like. He celebrated Mass in her parish church and gave her Communion. As for the other Theresa, Saint Thérèse of Lisieux, all the world knew of her. He went childlike to her as to a child, prayed at her Carmelite tomb, and met her sister Pauline—Mother Agnes of Jesus—another Carmelite. As for Nevers, it was a place wonderfully dear to him and to Maryknoll. It was there that was buried Our Lady's Saint Bernadette, who was also Father Price's Saint Bernadette. In the chapel where she lay, lay also Father Price's heart.

Then he returned to America, happy for his visits in Europe, but in health no stronger. The doctors ordered him—as he put it—to "loaf." On November 17 he wrote to his sister:

"I am continuing the 'loaf' treatment, leading something of a dog's life and being coddled as never before. If I don't come out of this a lazy man, I shall be surprised.

"Progress there is, though slow enough for one of my temperament. However, I am thankful for much. . . ."

He was totally unprepared to loaf, and he did not have to explain that fact as he did to his Maryknollers in his letter to them, far and wide, written on November 28:

"I was ordered 'to take the horizontal' as much as possible and to look forward to a period of comparative inactivity until Easter, when (unless some unforeseen trouble turns up) I should find myself better than I have been for years. After Christmas I must get into a warmer climate.

"That is the story in brief, and you may know that, after forty-two years of active priesthood, I find it a little difficult to 'loaf.' Happily the doctor has allowed me to carry on my desk work and Council sessions."

After Christmas, after he had been able to pontificate even at Midnight Mass, he was ordered not only to loaf but to go south—to Florida. He left the senior member of his Council as Acting General; he left his desk behind him.

Florida cured him no more than did Europe. So much did he hope that it might, that he almost deceived himself in thinking that it did. At the end of the winter he put on a bold face and started off to visit his houses in the West; but, before his train had whistled out of Florida, he had to leave it, and be carried to a Jacksonville hospital, Saint Vincent's. There was something wrong with his lungs.

From this hospital he wrote to his cousin, Mrs. Patrick Tracy, the daughter of his "second mother," Mrs. Daniel Shea:

"I have been basking in Florida sunshine since January, and, when presumably on my way to California, was held up by the medicos as a birthday present (February 24) and sentenced to stay here until Easter—for special treatment.

"You will be surprised to hear from me, although I think of you much oftener than you suspect.

"I write now because you—Patrick especially—will be interested to know that the Sister of Charity who personally watches my temperature, pulse, and so forth, was a Miss Harold. One day she asked me if I knew a Tracy family in Boston, and I then learned that she is a relative of Pat.

"She is a fine type, much beloved by all, especially by the nurses whom, as Superior, she has trained."

In March, 1935, he started north, and paused on the way at Raleigh, North Carolina, to visit the apostolic work which Father Price had once begun in North Carolina, and then for the sake of Maryknoll had dropped, but which now under Bishop Hafey had been revived. Father Price's North Carolina hills treated him well, better than Bavaria, better than Florida. He could mutter almost in surprise, "I feel better!"

By April he was back at Maryknoll and took his part in the Holy Week ceremonies, but not in the busier life of administration. He did ordain sixteen priests in June and did go to Clarks Summit—The Vénard—for the annual priests' retreat, and did preside at one more departure ceremony, but he could not deceive himself or others; except for a miracle, his life was over.

Just as he was becoming aware of this, he received a telegram more touching than its sender imagined. It was from Monsignor Francis X. Ford, Prefect Apostolic of the Kaying Prefecture in South China, who had once been Maryknoll's first student back in 1912. He was to be made bishop—Rome had spoken—even as his student companion at Maryknoll, James E. Walsh, had been made bishop. But Bishop James E. Walsh had been consecrated in China. Father Ford was to have the joy—or he begged for it—of being consecrated at Maryknoll by the surviving founder of Maryknoll. Father Ford did not know of the real condition of that founder, or of the exertion he was asking from him.

The receipt of this letter with its touching request did not restore Bishop Walsh's health, but it filled him with a determination to accomplish this consecration with his last strength, as a symbol of having completed his own life's cycle. On September 21, the Feast of Saint Matthew, the consecration would take place.

Long before that date he had to give up saying Mass with any regularity, and his walking had to be aided by a cane, yet he faced the day with a quiet confidence. It was a day God would grant to him as a day of strength by exception.

Maryknoll's chapel was still a so-called temporary one, a conference hall, and the ceremony could better take place in the chapel of the Motherhouse of the Maryknoll Sisters across

BISHOP WALSH'S LAST PUBLIC FUNCTION, THE
CONSECRATION OF BISHOP FORD

the road. The coconsecrators were Bishop Thomas E. Molloy, of Brooklyn, who, when an assistant in Saint John's Parish, Brooklyn, had encouraged the lad Francis Ford, with the Xavier in his name, to become a missioner; and Bishop Stephen J. Donahue, Auxiliary Bishop of New York, who had been young Francis Xavier Ford's classmate at Cathedral College, New York. At the entry of the sanctuary was stationed Doctor Sweet of Ossining, on the alert lest anything should happen to Bishop Walsh. But nothing did. From the moment that Mass began until its end, Bishop Walsh became stronger and stronger.

Then he retired, retired forever. There was no proper room for him in the Seminary; that is, not yet, for the apartment that should be his was in an uncompleted wing and was under construction. He had to lodge in the Motherhouse of the Sisters, in the "Bishop's Suite." When he celebrated Mass, there had to be a priest to help him. One day in October—the twenty-first—he drove in an automobile a hundred yards to his Seminary, to the quadrangle where took place the departure ceremonies. He could not dismount from his car, but he greeted all the students and priests individually, one after one, in friendly manner, with a smile and with attempts at quips. Then he looked at the new Seminary wing, and then at the statue of Our Lady under the kiosk, and, though always so restrained, he wept unrestrained tears.

On December 3, the Feast of Saint Francis Xavier, he made another journey, this time to the door of the Seminary, into which he was supported so that he could occupy the apartment that now was finished and now was his. For the next two days, as if to celebrate this return to his seminarians, he celebrated Mass, but not in public, ever in his private chapel. After that, no more Mass. After that, no more breviary, which never in all his priestly life he had omitted; only the rosary and various prayers and spiritual readings. The fall ordinations had been postponed in hopes of his recovery; but there was no recovery, and they were performed by the new Maryknoll missionary bishop, Bishop Francis X. Ford, on the eve of the Feast of The Immaculate Conception. After the ceremony Bishop Walsh insisted on having the new deacons brought to him so that he could congratulate them, which he did with sparkling eyes and ready tongue. Perhaps this asked of him too great an exertion. Certainly on the next day, the great Feast Day, December 8, he seemed to be like a candle fading. Father Cotta—*Father Foto*—was called to anoint him.

Bishop Walsh did not die on the Feast of The Immaculate Conception, December 8, or on December 25, Christmas. On Christmas he was able to listen to the students singing hymns for him in the corridor outside his room—singing his own hymn, "Only a Veil." But it was not he who celebrated the Midnight Mass in his private chapel, nor was it he—it was another bishop, Bishop Ford—who sang the Pontifical Mass in the Seminary chapel. He was living, but he had entered into that darkness where he could work no more.

Bishop Ford departed for China. In February news came to Bishop Walsh that one of the Maryknoll missioners had been captured by bandits in Manchukuo, Father J. Clarence Burns. The previous year Father Bush had been captured and held for three months. As yet there had been no violent death met by his Maryknoll missioners, but some day the martyrdoms would come, almost as surely as death was now coming to him.

He had come to such a state of helplessness that news that required action was not brought to him; only that about which nothing could be done, such as death. Father Kress, a Maryknoll missioner who had labored in Maryknoll missions of Los Angeles and Hawaii, died. Doctor Thomas P. Phelan, who for twenty-one years had been teaching Ecclesiastical History to the Maryknoll students, died. Maryknoll was losing these men, but not God. God was giving them activity, or granting them repose. All Bishop Walsh could do was to lie abed, fingering a rosary. He was like a child told to rest. Others were working.

No, there was one day when he was made to feel active. It was March first; on that day he had received the oaths of two Maryknoll Brothers. He had once again acted as the Superior General.

On March 23 Archbishop McNicholas visited him, and wrote later to Bishop Keough of Providence, telling of how he had found this helpless founder of Maryknoll:

"I thought to save him by making my visits brief and by limiting discussion to a few matters, but this was not his wish. His conversation took in the whole range of the Catholic Church, as was his custom. He made me feel that these would be his last opportunities to talk matters over with me. His mind was as keen, and his interest in the varied activities of the Church as great, as ever. . . .

"Bishop Walsh seemed to have no anxiety regarding his Society. He was profoundly grateful to Almighty God that so many good young men had given their lives to Maryknoll. He was not disturbed about laying down his burden, feeling that the devoted and capable young men would carry on the work of his Society. With paternal solicitude he feared that some of its members were taxing themselves beyond their strength."

Archbishop McNicholas wished to treat him as one still active—it is a courtesy to the sick. He asked him to jot down some notes of reminiscence concerning the late Archbishop Dowling of Saint Paul, in order that some one might write an appreciation of that prelate. This was one thing that Bishop Walsh could still do—write. He did not merely jot down notes. He wrote a well-composed article on Archbishop Dowling, on his seminary days with him at Brighton, and on the influence of the Abbé Hogan. He could still pay some debts to the past, even though the future was in other hands.

In payment of the same debt, he composed letters to all his Maryknoll family, letters not to be delivered to them until after his death.

My dear Sisters:

"Before leaving earth, let me acknowledge that I owe to your community no small portion of the success which has been credited to Maryknoll. Your generous and capable services and, above all, your constant prayers, have been with Maryknoll from the beginning. No one knows this better than I, and no one should be more grateful.

"I leave with you the affection of a father for his daughters, my one regret being that in these later years I could not know you individually as I would.

"It is a comforting thought that Mother Mary Joseph is being spared for your guidance and inspiration. May God keep her strong for many years to come!

"I hardly need to ask your prayers—you will give them

for me, I am sure. Mine for you will be that each of you may remain simple, generous, cheerful, and selfless, loving God and His saints with a strong personal affection, as little children love good parents.

"May God bless and keep you!

"Affectionately in Christ,"

✠ JAMES ANTHONY WALSH

To the Brothers of Maryknoll, whose devoted services he so well appreciated, the Maryknoll Superior wrote as follows:

"To our Auxiliary Brothers, wherever stationed, I write as father to sons, asking their frequent remembrance and assuring them always of what help I may be able to give them until they reach the goal that I am nearing.

"I have had a special pride in our Auxiliary Brothers—in their number and their quality. Their contribution to Maryknoll has been most valuable, not simply for material service, generously and intelligently rendered, but for their spiritual cooperation—sacrifices, prayers, Communion remembrances, and trials patiently borne for love of Christ and souls.

"May God keep each and all of our dear Brothers faithful to the highest ideals as followers of Christ!

"I leave you my blessing and the pledge of my affection.

"Devotedly in Christ,"

✠ JAMES ANTHONY WALSH

To young students at the novitiate at Bedford was written:

DEAR SONS IN CHRIST:

"I have longed to see you but I must be patient till, by God's grace, we meet in heaven.

"You are well entered on a year that should and will make

you know yourselves better and realize more fully the God-given task that lies before you. May this year of grace bring you very close to Christ and find you with a full purpose to seek His Will in all things—be it in life or death! Let Him be your tower of strength. 'I can do all things in Him who strengtheneth me.'

"Cultivate reliance on the Providence of God, and note His action on our lives and the lives of those dear to us. You will at times be astounded.

"I cannot urge you too strongly to keep humble. The self-opinionated man accomplishes little and is a disturbing influence. Try to see in others their point of view, and remember that arguments, unless sincerely used to get at the truth, are of little or no use.

"From the very beginning of your life as Maryknollers, respect your Superiors, as such. They may not always measure up to your ideal in every respect, but they represent God from whom our authority comes.

"Be generous, self-forgetting, and patient now, so that your later life as successful missioners will be assured.

"Pray often for me, and know that as God gives me power to plead for you, I will make use of it.

"Devotedly your father in Christ,"

✠ JAMES ANTHONY WALSH

To the seminarians at Maryknoll, the Father of the family wrote:

DEAR SONS IN CHRIST:

"The sands are going down in the glass, and my days are evidently numbered.

"It has been my privilege—a rare one for a cofounder—to see the work of Maryknoll developed to a promising maturity. I thank God for the opportunity and for the bountiful Providence which from the beginning has been so strikingly manifest.

"I am far from thinking that our development is perfect. No one has been more conscious of weakness than I, who for all these years have been at the head of our Society. I have often lamented my own shortcomings and my limitations. All that I can say for myself is that I have tried to be the willing instrument of God, who has urged me forward, leaving to me the duty of watching that I should not trip.

"The spirit of Maryknoll is often praised—at times much over-estimated—but we who hear the kindly word, while regretting that we do not reach the ideal, may yet be heartened as we are humbled.

"You, dear sons in Christ, have the future of Maryknoll in your keeping. That future will be secure if you remain humble, with childlike faith serving God and others for God, from the simple motive of love. *Primum Regnum Dei!* I have no fear for the future, if Maryknollers, in all their actions and discussions, will forget self and keep in mind the will and glory of God.

"May each of you persevere in his holy vocation and fight manfully to the end against worldliness and the powers of darkness!

"I leave you to our Heavenly Father; to Christ, our mission leader; to the Holy Ghost, our light and strength; and to the loving Mother of us all, Mary, most humble, Queen of Heaven.

"Keep me in your prayers, and look to me for what help it may be in my power to give you.

"Devotedly your father in Christ,"

✠ James Anthony Walsh

To the priests of the Society, he wrote:

Dear Priestly Sons in Christ:

"I make no distinction, since we are all missioners. Whether our daily tasks are in the homeland or on the field, we are of one heart and one mind, pledged to the evangelization of the world, with special interest in the people entrusted to our care by Rome.

"I write in the expectation of my own departure, this time, with God's grace, for the life that changes not. You have been my comfort, my pride, and my joy. I am fully aware that while much credit has been given to me, because of my position in the Society, my work would have been a failure without the help you have so generously given me.

"I have known my limitations, and you have borne with them. God certainly uses the weak for His divine purposes. But, after all, our work is His work, and you will make no mistake if you look to Him for guidance. All that He seeks from you is generosity and ready willingness to use the opportunities—or to meet the difficulties—which will inevitably present themselves.

"I have often urged you to appreciate what is good in other Societies than ours. Keep up this spirit, but watch closely that loyalty shall be a shining virtue in your life—loyalty to the Society, to your Superiors, to one another. That we may be one in Christ, is my prayer.

"Keep me in filial remembrance and know that, if God finds me worthy, I will be your helper until we meet merrily in heaven.

"Affectionately in Christ,"

✠ JAMES ANTHONY WALSH

It was April now, and there was sunshine, and it was a pleasure to him to be bolstered up in bed, so that he could see the Maryknoll students at their hour of recreation, on the terrace-like field between him and the Hudson. He could not feel young again, not even in the warmth that came from the sunlight streaming on his bed, but he could rejoice in the youth of others, especially those who were Maryknoll's future. He was looking at all life as through a window, all this mortal life.

He knew that Archbishop McNicholas was initiating a widespread campaign of prayer in his behalf, through appeals to the intercession of Blessed Martin de Porres. The Dominican Sisters throughout the country were praying for him. He was moved with gratitude. "It would be fine to see Blessed Martin add to the luster of his name by a good deed in my behalf," he wrote to the Archbishop; but as for his own wishes, "So far as I am personally concerned, I prefer to remain indifferent on the point and to let it be entirely a matter of God's will."

He preferred either to die or to become so well that he could go on with his work. As for lying this way, looking out of a window—it was not so much his choice. Yet it might be God's.

Holy Week began on April 5. On Holy Thursday Father Cotta once more anointed him. On Good Friday a Sister asked him how he felt. He smiled: "Oh, as right as anyone has a right to feel on Good Friday."

To Mother Mary Joseph he confided: "With Saint Paul I keep saying, I rejoice in my sufferings and fill up those things that are wanting of the sufferings of Christ in my flesh."

Holy Saturday dawned, but without true dawning; a meager, gray, biting day.

Easter dawned. It brought no sunlight in the sky, and no ray of hope that the Bishop could continue much longer as a Maryknoller at Maryknoll. The doctors had long since found a shadow on his right lung. Now his left lung was involved. He could not breathe. His coughing was a torture to him and to those who heard.

So likely did it seem that he would die on Easter that someone whispered to him that it was a good time to die. The Bishop was just strong enough to smile and ask if the Feast of the Ascension would not also be a good time.

He did not die on Easter, or on Easter Monday. It was on Easter Tuesday that took place his departure. Early in the morning he received Holy Communion as his Viaticum. "Frequently he lifted his arms and exclaimed 'God!' varying this with the ejaculation, 'Jesus, Mary, Joseph!' "

At ten o'clock the Maryknoll priests were called in; they gave their blessing and retired to the adjoining chapel to remain for their Father General in his hour of death. And death came at twenty-seven minutes past ten. It was April 14, 1936. "Jesus, Mary, Joseph!"

The Sleeper in Christ

WE HAVE it on the authority of Saint Thomas More that proud men of his day, who thought that they had cut quite a figure in this life, liked to have a preview of their own funerals. They liked to imagine themselves peering from the windows of their own houses down at their own funeral processions. Look at the superb black horses, black-caparisoned, with silver trimmings! Look at the crowd! But—even more—look at the dignitaries! It was almost worth-while to die in order to be honored by such a pageant.

Bishop Walsh did not try to comfort his dying days by staring at his own funeral cortege. It was not the habit, even among proud men, in his day so to do—they had little taste for pageantry, none for pageantry around a corpse, and they were much more ready to steal a preview of their obituary notices in the morning newspapers. And he was not proud. And he was too canny to try to beguile himself, in an important moment of his life, with anything so unimportant as his own self-importance. He did give careful instructions as to how he should be dressed in his coffin, for he wanted things to be done right and followed his own dictum: "Leave nothing at loose ends."

He had planned conscientiously, as one wishing to take the load from others to the last, where and how he should be buried. There would be for him a Solemn Mass at Maryknoll, and then interment in the quiet terrace at the northwest of the Seminary, up to which the trees marched from a ravine out of which in his first days at Sunset Hill he had had to cart water. It was a green, sequestered shelf, reminiscent of some of the happier recesses in the flank of the mountain which Dante climbed to his earthly paradise. It balanced the recreation field to the south of the Seminary, and was as quiet and secluded as the recreation field was at times noisy and lively with batted balls.

He had staked out this retreat for Maryknoll's cemetery, and had cut away a bank to make it level, and had turfed it, and had there buried a dozen Maryknollers—priests, Brothers, Sisters—and to watch over them had set up a great wooden cross on which hung Our Lord in bronze. It was a corner so tranquil that the wild rabbits came there regularly to nibble green grass between the dandelions, and would not be scared away even by the visitors who came there to spade or to pray.

The funeral which actually took place was quite other than he had planned, although his resting place was to be the rabbit-haunted cemetery. A pageant was presented to him that even the pageant-loving Londoner of 1500 would have given his life for. It was Cardinal Hayes who caused it to take place by asking that the Solemn Mass of Requiem be celebrated in his Saint Patrick's Cathedral, which still towered, Gothic and impressive, above Fifth Avenue—down which the full divisions of Pershing's army had paraded in 1919 at platoon front while Maryknoll's army of four had been going, squad right, to China—the lace work of its towers looking up at the riveters on the Rockefeller Center.

So on Thursday, after double ceremonies which took place at Sunset Hill, both at his Seminary and at the Motherhouse of Mother Mary Joseph's Sisters of Saint Dominic, the body was carried to New York, accompanied by a police escort. During Thursday night the Sisters of *Bon Secours,* whose custom and privilege was being respected, prayed beside his body in Saint Patrick's Cathedral, the doors of which were locked.

On Friday began the episcopal pomp. Only a small corner in the Cathedral could be allotted to laymen, so many religious, so many priests, had to have their precedence. It was scarcely light before the space reserved for laymen had been occupied. Then into the nave to take their places in the pews to the right trooped six hundred Sisters, representatives of thirty-five communities. The Maryknoll Sisters, one hundred and thirty-five of them, had the position of honor next to the casket as its guard. After that filed in from the sacristy six hundred ecclesiastics—five hundred of them priests, thirty-five of them Monsignors, fifteen of them bishops, three of them archbishops, and one of them a Cardinal, Cardinal Hayes.

The Cardinal presided at the Solemn Pontifical Mass. Archbishop Mooney, of Rochester, was the celebrant, with Father James F. Kelly as deacon, and Father Winslow of Maryknoll's Council as subdeacon.

And he for whom the Mass was being celebrated lay in body in the midst of this array of the Church militant, in a coffin of walnut wood. On the finger of the white-mitered dead

Bishop still stayed the ring which Pope Pius XI had presented to him on his consecration; it was to be buried with his body. In his hands had been set the crucifix that once had belonged to Father Price, which was not to be buried.

From the rank of archbishops rose, in due time, Archbishop McNicholas to deliver the eulogy.

He began by describing the end of this Bishop who now slept in Christ: "The night of his life came upon him, one might say, unexpectedly. He had toiled joyously through a laborious day. He thought not of the gains made, but with more than human prudence mapped out for himself and his colaborers the work providentially entrusted to his Society."

"With more than human prudence." It was an emphatic phrase. Archbishop McNicholas, in thanking God for the life and work of Bishop Walsh, could not help lauding his life and work and character, yet he was not one of those panegyrists who rise to eloquence by superlative flattery. The phrase, "with more than human prudence," had been carefully chosen, and it stood out like a high light in a picture classically painted. There was another phrase which revealed why the Archbishop considered that the deceased Bishop had been able to enjoy such a prudence. It was the only phrase in the address that applied the title "saint" even indirectly to his friend: "His trust in Divine Providence seemed to me that of a saint."

There were many virtues which the Archbishop went on to attribute to Bishop Walsh: "dauntless courage," "keenness of mind," "gentle firmness," "decision of character," all of which were to be admired. But some of his qualities aroused not only

A WREATH ON THE GRAVES OF THE COFOUNDERS OF MARYKNOLL, IN THE MARYKNOLL CEMETERY

urer General, read his report. He said, speaking of the late
Bishop and Superior General: "He had completed the material foundations necessary for the Society's work. . . . At his
going we were free of serious commercial debt, and untram-
meled by financial servitude." Then also, almost as a matter
of parenthesis, he remarked, "Father General's task was not
unfinished."

This was a tribute to the habit of Bishop Walsh of leaving
"nothing up in the air." He always finished his day's work.
His desk was never left in disorder with the unattended-to. A
successor might at any moment have stepped into his position
and found every paper in its place.

It was also a tribute to how much in his lifetime he had accomplished. He had builded Maryknoll at home and in the
Far East. He had not merely begun to launch our country on
its missionary destiny, which it had derived from the very
voyage of Columbus: he had launched it thoroughly, so that
there was no turning back.

But implicitly the statement attested to something even more
fundamental. Bishop Walsh had done nothing by halves. He
had not merely by halves given himself to God's will. He had,
as a boy, opened his eyes to the light; and as a priest he had
taken up the task which that light presented to him, which
was to give light to others. His fulfillment of his work was not
measured by how far he had carried his labors, but by the
fullness with which he had made himself a part of that light
and a cooperator with God's will.

"Till the shadows lengthen," had been the wording of Cardinal Newman's prayer, "and the evening comes, and the busy

world is hushed." His own daylight on earth had to have its ending, and it was part of his task to accept that earthly ending. "All the day long" he had labored, and now he was approaching his peace.

He had earned the title which had appeared on his bishop's shield, and which was later to be carved on his tombstone, *"Primum Regnum Dei."* He had finished the task of putting first in his life "God's Kingdom."

NOTES

1. *The Voice*, May, 1936, p. 37.
2. *A Modern Martyr*, Maryknoll, N. Y., 1913, p. 47.
3. *Ibid.*, p. 165.
4. *Ibid.*, p. 198.
5. Address by Maryknoll Superior to Maryknoll Novices' Unit, Catholic Students' Mission Crusade, 1924.
6. Guilday, *The Pastorals of the American Hierarchy—1792-1919*, Washington, 1923, p. 263.
7. Memorial of Father André.
8. Address by Maryknoll Superior to Maryknoll Novices' Unit, Catholic Students' Mission Crusade, 1924.
9. *American Catholics and Foreign Missions:* address delivered to the Eighth National Convention of Catholic Students' Mission Crusade, 1933, J. A. Walsh, p. 4.
10. *The Field Afar*, December, 1907, p. 11.
11. *The Voice*, May, 1936, p. 37.
12. *The Sacred Heart Review*, November 18, 1905, p. 331.
13. *In the Homes of Martyrs*, Maryknoll, N. Y., 1922, p. 70.
14. *The Field Afar*, April-May, 1910, p. 3.
15. *The Sacred Heart Review*, April 10, 1909, p. 259.
16. Cf. *Sermons and Addresses*, Vol. III, p. 144, *First Missionary Congress*, F. C. Kelly, Chicago, 1909, p. 364.
17. Cardinal O'Connell, *Recollections of Seventy Years*, Houghton Mifflin Co., 1934, p. 63.

18. *The Field Afar*, June-July, 1911, p. 2.
19. *Ibid.*, May, 1936, p. 151.
20. *Ibid.*, February-March, 1912, p. 7.
21. *Ibid.*, April-May, 1912, p. 6.
22. *Maryknoll Chronicle*, p. 106.
23. *Ibid.*, p. 114.
24. *The Field Afar*, June-July, 1912, p. 5.
25. *Ibid.*, April-May, 1912, p. 6.
26. *Ibid.*, December, 1912, p. 5.
27. *Ibid.*, December, 1912, p. 6.
28. *Ibid.*, December, 1912, p. 9.
29. *Ibid.*, April, 1913, p. 4.
30. *Ibid.*, May, 1913, p. 13.
31. *Ibid.*, April, 1913, p. 11.
32. *Ibid.*, December, 1912, p. 6.
33. *Ibid.*, December, 1913, p. 11.
34. McShane, Rev. John Francis, *My Brother—The Maryknoll Missionary*, St. Meinrad, Ind., 1932, p. 34.
35. *Maryknoll Chronicle*, p. 343.
36. *Observations in the Orient*, Maryknoll, N. Y., 1919, p. 21.
37. *Ibid.*, p. 32.
38. *Ibid.*, p. 50.
39. *Ibid.*, p. 74.
40. *Ibid.*, p. 43.
41. *Ibid.*, p. 104.
42. *Ibid.*, p. 109.
43. *Ibid.*, p. 119.
44. *Ibid.*, pp. 196-197.
45. *Maryknoll Mission Letters*, Vol. I, 1923, p. 62.
46. Circular Letter, April 17, 1922.
47. *Ibid.*
48. *Ibid.*
49. Letter of the Superior to Missioners, April 22, 1921, Maryknoll Archives.
50. Letter of January, 1928.
51. Easter, 1912.
52. *The Field Afar*, March, 1929, p. 75.
53. F. L. Allen's *Since Yesterday*, New York, 1910, p. 75.

54. Letter of August 11, 1930.

55. Eulogy by Father Callan.

56. *The Field Afar,* March, 1931, p. 77.

57. *Ibid.,* April, 1932, p. 102.

58. *Maryknoll Mission Letters,* Vol. II, 1927, p. 16.

59. *Ibid.,* p. 34.

60. *The Field Afar,* December, 1932, p. 342.

61. *Ibid.,* December, 1931, p. 335.

62. Letter of March 3, 1931.

63. Letter of May 8, 1931.

64. *The Field Afar,* September, 1931, p. 241.

65. Letter of September 11, 1931.

66. *The Field Afar,* December, 1932, p. 343.

67. Letter on Feast of The Immaculate Conception, 1932.

68. Letter of September, 1932.

69. *The Field Afar,* July-August, 1933, p. 214.

70. Eulogy by Father Callan.

71. From *Fides News Service,* reprinted in *The Field Afar,* October, 1933, pp. 276-277.

72. Letter to Fathers McHugh and Callan, August 10, 1933.

73. *The Field Afar,* May, 1936, pp. 131-132.